CW01338411

signposts

signposts
Bengali Poetry Since Independence

EDITED BY
Prabal Kumar Basu

ADVISORS
Kalyani Ghose
Jogen Chowdhury
Samik Bandopadhyay
Sunil Gangopadhyay
Nirmal Kanti Bhattacharjee

Rupa & Co

Copyright © Prabal Kumar Basu 2002

Published 2002 by

Rupa & Co

7/16, Ansari Road, Daryaganj
New Delhi 110 002

Offices at:
15 Bankim Chatterjee Street, Calcutta 700 073
135 South Malaka, Allahabad 211 001
PG Solanki Path, Lamington Road, Mumbai 400 007
36, Kutty Street, Nungambakkam, Chennai 600 034
Surya Shree, B-6, New 66, Shankara Park,
Basavangudi, Bangalore 560 004
3-5-612, Himayat Nagar, Hyderabad 500 029

ISBN 81-7167-639-1

All rights reserved.
No part of this publication may be
reproduced, stored in a retrieval system,
or transmitted in any form or by any means,
electronic, mechanical, photocopying,
recording or otherwise, without
the prior permission of the publishers.

Book Design & Typeset by
Arrt Creations
45 Nehru Apts Kalkaji
New Delhi 110 019
arrt@vsnl.com

Printed in India by
Rekha Printers Pvt Ltd
A 102/1
Okhla Industrial Area - Phase II
New Delhi 110020

Dedicated to

The readers whose interest in

Bengali poetry breaks the barrier of language

Contents

Foreword   xvii

Prologue   xxi

Arun Mitra
(1909-2000)

At The Sight Of The Smoke	1
These Few Lines	2
The One Who's Come	3

Subhas Mukhopadhyay
(1919)

The Man Never Found Out	4
I Am Miserable	5
The Knight Check	7
My Work	9
To Hangers On	10

Birendra Chattopadhyay
(1920-1985)

In The Meeting Of Poets	11
The Amazing Smell Of Rice in the Night Sky	12
Behula's Raft	13
Headless Trunks Scream In Glee	14

Arun Sarkar
(1922-1980)

Naren Master	15
Destitute	16
Father	17
A summer Poem	18

Nirendranath Chakrabarty
(1924)

All Kinds Of Loving	19
The Palace	21
It's So At Times	22
Seeing It Through To The End	23
Jesus Of Calcutta	25

Manindra Gupta
(1926)

Ashtray	27
The Pilot	28
The Candle	29

Sarat Kumar Mukhopadhyay
(1931)

To My Friend's Wives	30
Bending Down And Down	31
Sounds	32
Birajmohan	33

Aloke Sarkar
(1931)

Secret Abode	34
Which Way Is Heaven	35
Everyday He Watches	37
See	39

Shankha Ghosh
(1932)

Babu Says	43
Beautiful	44
A Big Fool, Unsocial Too	46
Idle Water	47
The Decade	48

Alokeranjan Dasgupta
(1933)

The Blood Stained Lattice Window	49
The Late Afternoon Sky	50
The Evening Press Conference	51
Roads Lost In Temples And Mosques	52

Shakti Chattopadhyay
(1933-1995)

Jarasandha	53
Pleading Portrait	54
Unruly I Roam	55
O Forever Venerable Fire	56
That Isn't Time For Much Joy — That Isn't Time For Much Happiness	57

Sunil Gangopadhyay
(1934)

Nineteen Seventy One	59
A City Of Memories	61
For Che Guevera	62
Neera's Illness	64
The Nurse-Maid	66

Benoy Majumdar
(1934)

Me And My Oleander Flower	68
Can Give You Love	69
Last Evening	70
Yet Some More Time	71

Tushar Roy
(1934-1977)

Check And See	72
Then	73
Who Is The Hunter	74
A Poem Dedicated To The Beloved	75

Samarendra Sengupta (1935)	The Stairs Of Coffee House	76
	Quarter To Twelve	78
	He Came And Stood	80
Amitava Dasgupta (1935)	The Wooden Chair	82
	I Am India	84
	Poetry And Slogan	87
	Dhaka May 21:1990	88
Utpal Kumar Basu (1936)	Demon	90
	Breadcrumbs Off My Shirt	91
	The Ship Sailing Away	90
	My Spectral Spirit	94
Pranabendu Dasgupta (1936)	About Houses	95
	It Is Time For Me To Go	98
	The Quarrel	99
	Who-Whom	100
Tarapada Roy (1936)	On Some Days I Feel sad	101
	What Was It That I Wanted	102
	The Indian Map	103
	The Cooling Machine	104
Shaktipada Brahmachari (1937)	The Fowler	105
	Pour Femme	106
	Conference Of Poets	107

ix

Vijaya Mukhopadhyay
(1937)

All this Play-Acting	111
Advertisement	112
Equation	113
Out Of Raghuvamsha	114

Manibhusan Bhattacharya
(1938)

Montu's Day	115
The Story Of The Martyr's Day	118
Night At Gandhinagar	120

Pabitra Mukhopadhyay
(1940)

He Who Is Alone	121
To A Dead Friend	122
Politics	123
Of Defeated Humanity	125

Geeta Chattopadhyay
(1941)

My Being: Embryo	127
Birth	128
Ocean To Himalayas	129
Burning Of The Sati	130

Piyush Raut
(1941)

You Too, God	131
The Prelude To Revolution	132
About Him	133

Bhaskar Chakrabarty
(1945)

When Will Winter Come, Suparna	134
For The Lost Youth	136
Another Love Poem	137
Death	138

Debarati Mitra | Motion | 141
(1946) | Applied Mathematics | 142
 | No, No And No | 144

Amitava Gupta | Omega Point | 145
(1947) | Bengali | 146
 | Arjun: To Karna | 147
 | Yudhistir: To Kunti | 148

Krishna Basu | Hymn To The Goddess | 149
(1947) | A Woman's Corpse | 150
 | Your Girlchild | 151
 | Just An Ordinary Mail | 152

Ranajit Das | April | 154
(1949) | International | 155
 | To My Father | 156
 | Smile For The Camera | 157

Tushar Chaudhury | Hunting Ground | 158
(1949) | Seducing Beautiful Nina | 159
 | O Life Eternal | 161
 | The Night Wears On | 162

Parthapratim Kanjilal | To Friends | 163
(1949) | More Poems Of The Night | 164
 | Table | 165

Shyamalkanti Das (1951)	The Four Friends	166
	Allegory	168
	O My Motherland	170
	With Wood	171
Joy Goswami (1954)	Funeral Verses	172
	Maltibala School For Girls'	174
	Victorious	176
	The Future Missing Girl	179
	Hawk Of Iron, For You	180
Dhiman Chakrabarty (1954)	Rope	182
	Doleful	183
	Arms	184
Punnyasloke Dasgupta (1955)	Fornication	185
	Cunning	186
	Love	187
Mridul Dasgupta (1955)	The Blindness After Sunset	188
	Woman Thy Name Is Desire	189
	Mishap	190
	Solution In Simplicity	191
Subodh Sarkar (1957)	Gandhi	192
	Sari	194
	How To Be A Good Communist	196
	The Kind Of Wife We Want	197

Sanjukta Bandopadhyay (1958)

Pill	201
The She-Cat	202
In This Birth As a Woman	203
The Geometry We Could Not Learn	204

Aneek Rudra (1959)

Apocalypse	206
Incarnation Of Dwarf	208
The Portrait Of Living	209

Pinaki Thakur (1959)

Generation	211
Girl-Friend Dear	212
Passenger	214

Jahar Sen Majumdar (1960)

Signal	215
Ladder	216
Back Of One's Head	217

Mallika Sengupta (1960)

Open Letter To Freud	218
Tell Us Marx	220
A Mark Of Blood	221
A Fish Whip In The Feudal Age	222

Prabal Kumar Basu (1960)

By My Personal Memorial	223
Living Scape	225
Rhino	227
The Wall	228

Joydev Basu
(1962)

India : A Search	231
Twenty-Seventh Birthday	233
Arowal Or Kansara Or...	234
For Comrade Musa Mollah	235

Rahul Purakayastha
(1963)

Poem Of 12 Noon	237
Open Jaws	238
Mask	239

Rupak Chakrabarty
(1965)

Twenty-Fifth Baisakh	240
Fish	241
The White Letter	242

Chiranjib Basu
(1968)

The Uncertain Path	243
A Dream Originated Dialogue	244
Pilgrimage	245

Bibhas Roychaudhury
(1969)

The Archer	246
Rice	247
My Dear Father	248

Mandrakanta Sen
(1972)

A Strange Affair	250
Alone In Moon City	252
When Just You	253

The Poets — 257

The Artists — 265

Glossary

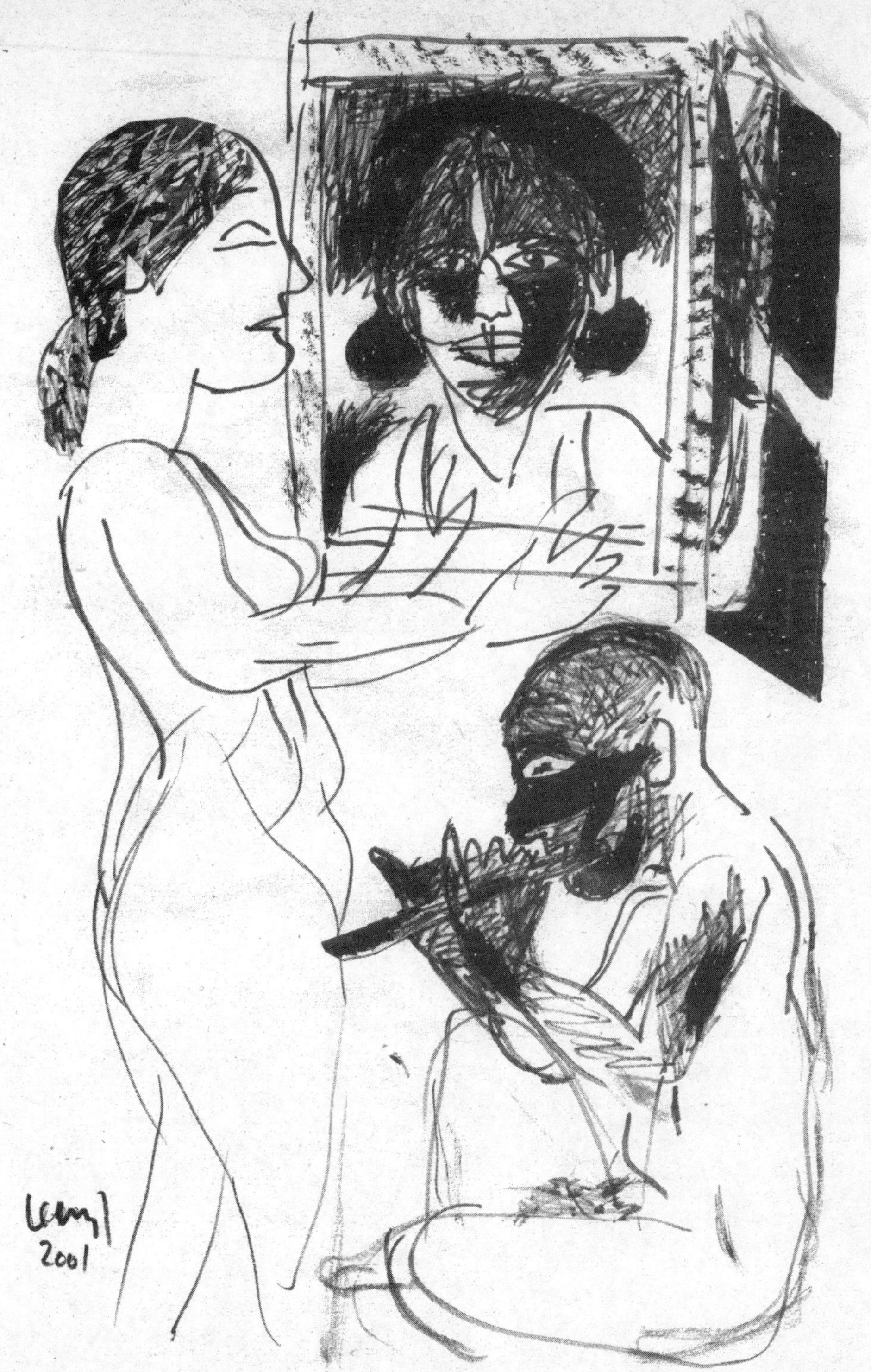
2001

FOREWORD

Bengali as a language though currently graded the fifth among other major world languages, the world outside is quite unaware of the literary endeavours in Bengali. Bengali speaking people are known to reside all over the expanse of the world, as a community they are fairly well known to the cosmopolitan genre. But the identity of a community remains obscure till one is conscious of its language, literature and culture. Even those who know the name of Rabindranath Tagore outside this subcontinent, or often read him in translation, do not always know the name of the first language of his works. For them Rabindranath is an Indian (of undivided India) poet, and in many countries mistakenly labeled as a Hindu poet. During the lifetime of Rabindranath, due to the aura of his genius, Bengali language could reach an eminence of its own, but after him, we his successors, unfortunately could not defend the honour.

Three of the five major world languages are Oriental. In comparison to these, i.e. Chinese, Hindi and Bengali, the other two European languages English and Spanish have earned a lot more literary acclaim and at the same time enjoy much greater readership. It is needless to say that English Literature is rich with its variety of contents and Spanish Literature particularly in the second half of the twentieth century has won over the world. But it will be unfortunate if the Oriental languages are identified merely as the languages being spoken by millions of people around the world.

After the Middle Ages the daring Europeans started exploring in their warships the hitherto unknown world and began to establish their empires and colonies in the newfound lands. Along with economic exploitation, they started spreading and implanting their language and religion. With the onset of the new age, mass uprising, freedom struggle gained ground and the ruling class were forced to break up their empires, Europeans had to leave the colonies, but by then they had created a long lasting abode for their language and religion. Spain is not one of the big powers at the moment, but Spanish is the foremost language in the entire South America, barring just a few countries. The Spanish writers of South America are far more famous than the writers from Spain itself. The situation is almost similar with the British. They are weakened considerably after the downsizing of their empire, and ironically have to court America, once a colony of the British. The American English writers too have much greater dominance today than the British writers do.

The eastern countries never tried to expand their empire afar, not necessarily because they were peace loving, on the contrary because of their fear and ignorance of the ocean. Some say, the wood which is necessary for building large sturdy ships, like oak was unavailable in these countries. Chengiz Khan the founder of the largest empire of the world had proved his might only on land. The powerful Chinese emperors never thought of conquering Australia, just across the sea. The Mughals of India, who had surpassed the Europeans in both might and wealth for a few centuries even did not dare to venture across the waters. The Mughal Empire got weakened with time, as the rulers could not adapt themselves to the changing era. Foreign invaders routed China. Gradually for some centuries the eastern countries slumped under the curse of slavery, poverty and illiteracy. Under the influence of the diminutive countries of Europe, many of the native dialects, local culture of the African and the two American countries have nearly been obliterated. They have lost their cultural heritage. But the ancient traditions of China or India were so deep-rooted that no foreign aggression could wipe it out. On the contrary some intellectuals of the ruling community, fascinated by the Indian Art and Culture, engaged themselves in the study of the same.

One great advantage of China is that the Chinese people are bound by one common language. Indians speak in many languages, practise diverse modes of subsistence. The character of each community thus formed due to linguistic difference is miles apart from each other. Despite such disparities, it is amazing how India has been successfully been able to tie together the heterogeneous ethnic groups.

Bengali is one of the major languages, which was born of the Indo-European language family through Sanskrit and Latin. Though the languages have branched out intricately, Bengali is the far removed relative of German and English. Bengali is the youngest in this family of languages. Considering it to be a thousand years old, barring a few patches here and there in the intermediate centuries, Bengali has really flowered in the last three centuries and by far has surpassed most of the other Indian languages in its prosperity. Kolkata had been the power centre of the British and the Bengalis were exposed to the modern world through English. At the embryonic stage, apart from the osmotic inputs of modernism, it grew under the tutelage of such gigantic genius as Bankim Chandra Chattopadhyay, who had accumulated the best from both Sanskrit and English. And immediately afterwards Rabindranath emerged as the rising sun not only in poetry, but demonstrated amazing virtuosity in short stories, novels, plays, essays and songs too. These two had taken Bengali literature to such a height that this was a tremendous onus on their successors to maintain it.

After Rabindranath, the next generation writers continued to be fascinated by his merit, but could still come out of his thought processes, his form and strove to create a new dimension in literature. This has shaped Bengali literature as a fast moving, bouncing river of movement towards the future era. In Bengali poetry Jibanananda Das stood in one of the bends of such a river from where Rabindranath was no longer visible. Jibanananda Das and his contemporaries have enriched Bengali Poetry from the time prior to the Second World War till nearly a decade after our Independence. Many more streams have flourished since then. This Anthology endeavours to emphasize on the contemporary poets. Arun Mitra who was the oldest passed away very recently and was creative till his last breath. Subhas Mukhopadhyay and Nirendranath Chakrabarty, though ripe in age, are intimately involved in writing poetry. Some of the most eminent poets have had untimely deaths but their creations are still significant. The majority of the poets included in this collection are young, the youngest being Mandakranta Sen who is in her late twenties. We can perhaps take a legitimate pride in the fact that for the first time we have come out with an anthology in English which boasts of the youthful brilliance of Bengali poetry.

Sunil Gangopadhyay
Kolkata, November 2001

PROLOGUE

The latter half of the twentieth century is significant for several reasons. The first half of the century was dominated by the Russian revolution, spread of communism, the spectacular advances in science and technology, producing more powerful weapons of destruction and offering fresh prospects of creation at the same time. The paradigm shifted from the material world to one's inner psyche. This urge for introspection and self-consciousness along with the development of the electronic media in the second half of the last century had a deep impact on the sensibility and ethics of humanity. The centre of power gradually shifted towards economics. Politics came to prefer democracy to monarchy or dictatorship.

India did not remain unaffected by these tendencies. After two hundred years, in the middle of the twentieth century India was freed from the British Raj. This came about at a time when the British were in the process of slowly winding up their vast empire. But the invaluable independence of the country was earned only at the cost of splitting the country into two on religious lines. A new state, Pakistan, was born, with deep and long - lasting implications for both the countries.

Punjab and Bengal in India were the two states directly affected by this partition. Both were geographically severed, some portions of the erstwhile states now belonged to Pakistan. People in these parts of the country felt insecure and imperilled. Many could not associate themselves intimately to the new state. They had to forego their entire belongings of a lifetime to move into a new country as refugees. The affluent and socially well placed suddenly faced the perils and the trauma of the have-nots. A new struggle for existence had started for them.

In the wider perspective India's struggle for existence had also begun. India had to ensure the impregnability of her sovereignty and at the same time come of age. In the midst of all the shock, bewilderment, and despair there lurked a hope which actually helped to shape India to its present configuration. The history of metamorphosis has by now gone deep into our social structure, our thought processes and our expressions, as reflected in Indian culture, literature and art. The truncated Bengal witnessed a much greater impact of all these.

At the time of Independence in 1947, the province comprising the present West Bengal and the country Bangladesh was together known as Bengal. Lord Curzon had divided this into east and west Bengal at the beginning of the last century. The area marked as East Bengal became part of the new state of Pakistan after Partition. People of the same country, same soil, speaking the same language, with the same food habits, abruptly found themselves separated by barbed wires.

The majority of these people felt insecure and moved with meagre belongings to West Bengal as refugees. They now had to cope with a completely new life.

Yet another significant feature of post-Independent West Bengal has been the wide dissemination of the leftist ideas, which later in the sixties took a more radical direction in the Naxalite movement. It had far-reaching consequences politically and on the social milieu too. The main objective of the movement was to radically change the prevalent social system. Later the leftists changed or had to deviate from their stand and had to pragmatically modify themselves when they came to power in the late seventies and have continued to rule West Bengal since then. This is an exceptional instance when compared to the political character of the other states of the country.

A simultaneous inner evolution was silently transpiring, with the gradual slackening of the traditional human relationship that have constituted the core of Indian society. The more life became urbanized and industrialized, people were becoming more selfconscious. All thought tended to pivot around the self. The question of livelihood took centre stage. People were forced to move away from their roots on professional obligations, calling for a lot of adjustments. An overall alienation could be perceived. Deviousness was the outcome of this detachment. People took to deception. Masked faces paraded around.

Art and literature document the contemporary reality. Modern Bengali poetry grew out of and reflected this anxious, restless state. People talk about modern poetry being different from the earlier poetry. Some find it is less accessible, some call it difficult. But it is nothing extraordinary. Human beings are resistant to change, and naturally find it difficult to accept the modern directions in art and literature. One of the directions that Bengali poetry took in this phase amounted to a retraction from more conventional free play of the imagination and a creative negotiation with more impersonal image – making, with the vision extending beyond the seen and the physically existent. Poetry tended to become more predominantly confessional, with individual confession drawing on the collective, seeking to open up the hidden spaces in the stricken soul of the community. For Bengali poetry in the post-Independence period, modernism was defined in terms of this self–disclosure.

The present anthology tries to sketch the evolution of Bengali Poetry in a fast changing socio-economic milieu. Here Bengali Poetry signifies poetry written in the Republic of India only. This anthology endeavours to record the transitions in language, form, content and philosophy in post-Independent Bengali Poetry. The anthology also aims at projecting a well balanced and comprehensive view of Bengali poetry in the last half century to readers outside

West Bengal and even outside India, as evidence of the richness of one of the several regional literatures of India.

Right from the start we had decided to restrict the number of poets to fifty as we thought this would ideally represent the fifty years of Bengali poetry. This was not an easy job. We had to choose the representative poets, those who have made significant impact on Bengali literature. This of course does not mean that the poets not chosen have made no contribution at all. Nevertheless the effort has been to maintain an overall continuity. The selection has not been restricted to the state of West Bengal only; there are poems by poets in Assam and Tripura, writing in Bengali.

The next problem was to identify the poet with whom we could start the anthology. Though Madhusudan Dutt was the first modern Bengali poet his writings failed to create a real impact on his successors. It was with Rabindranath Tagore that Bengali poetry began to become modern in its totality. The post-Tagorean era can be rightfully called the era of modern poetry. The main poets in this gestation of modernism were Jibanananda Das, Sudhindranath Dutta, Bishnu Dey, Amiya Chakraborty, Buddhadev Basu, Samar Sen etc. They had all blossomed and established themselves as poets much before Independence, and still remained creative for more than a decade after Independence. However we decided to keep these great poets out of this anthology and include those poets whose creative maturity and recognition came after Independence. The decision was tough, but once taken made our work easier. The oldest poet of this anthology was born in 1909 and the youngest in 1972.

There is a prevalent system of locating poets in their respective decades according to the time span in which a particular poet had begun writing and came to be recognized. Thus the last fifty years of Bengali poetry could be divided into five decades with distinct traits. Poetic idiom, thought and philosophy have distinctive departures in each of the decades. Poems were selected primarily on the following three considerations:

a) that they should be chosen from the best works of the poet

b) that they should lend themselves to worthwhile translation

c) that they should reflect the distinctive character of the time

The collection begins with Arun Mitra. Like him Subhas Mukhopadhyay, Nirendranath Chakrabarty, Arun Sarkar and Birendra Chattopadhyay too had started their careers before Independence, but they have been included since they continued to yield considerable impact upon Bengali Poetry during the fifties and sixties also.

The fifties began with a dream ... the dream of building a new nation. A whole world of expectations. The dreams and the expectations gave birth to a kind of romanticism, made up of the vibrancy of the youth on the one hand, and doubts on the other. Distrust was still to come. Love was no longer a myth. Love sought to crack the myth apart and reach physicality. Everything centred on the city. The sense of helplessness that haunted the poets of the immediately preceding generation, the sense of political ineffectiveness that led them to burst into protest, the folk conventions that persisted half way towards urbanization and the cravings that marked them were conspicuously absent in the fifties. The poetic idiom was fast shedding all artifice to approximate to the colloquial. Everyday speech provided the staple of poetic diction.

At the time of independence in 1947, most of the poets of the post-fifties were either in their childhood or adolescence. In other words the excitement and thrill of the freedom movement had eluded them. But they had to bear the burden of the fall out. After a decade of freedom India was slowly coming of age. After the initial euphoria, people now were face to face with reality. The dawning of reality bred disbelief and turbulence, sharpening both self-consciousness and a passion for self discovery. The political parties were in the throes of internal discussion on ideological issues. The Communist Party of India was divided. The state witnessed the first armed political revolution ... the Naxalite movement. The inner conflicts and tensions that came with these developments led to a spirit of alienation in Bengali poetry ... an alienation that intensified the self-questioning that had already surfaced, and that would now manifest itself in a wide range of experimentation.

A rather controversial literary movement that took place within the span covered by the present anthology was the Hungry Movement in the sixties. Hungry from Hunger ... a hunger that oftened turned to the hunger of the senses, drawing the charge of obscenity against several of these works. Poetry faced the wrath of the police and the law. Many poets were put behind bars. The movement broke down under the onslaught and fizzled out. Another movement that gained momentum at around the same time was the 'Sruti' movement. It rallied for self-criticism or self-analysis. The poetry of the sixties tended to defy conventional metrics and adopt prose as a vehicle for poetry. The objective of this movement was to search for multifarious dimensions in a word, to make the audible and the visible complementary to each other. It sought the portrayal of an expression. The expression also underwent a thorough metamorphosis. Many a time the stress was on form, artistry.

Quite a few powerful poets were associated with these two movements. But in the ultimate analysis their works during this period failed to leave any definite impression. So no poem from these movements has been included in this collection.

One consolidation achieved in the seventies was the return of the native splendour of poetic metres in Bengali. The majority poets of the sixties in their predilection for different experimentations a la western Poetry, tended to neglect the metrical beauty of Bengali Poetry. The poets of the seventies however rediscovered this native genius and exploited it to its fullest potential.

The post-independence dream started cracking in the seventies. Pakistan faced another split. East Pakistan fought and won the battle for a separate state. During the liberation movement of Bangladesh a fresh lot of people had to abandon their belongings and flee to India again. The refugee problem took new dimensions. A disillusioned and confused people were driven to think on fresh lines. Decadence threatened the very existence of man. Poets took to satire.

Communist doctrines had aroused considerable interest long before Independence. The Marxist philosophy was naturally reflected in several poems. Sheer Romanticism no longer held sway. It was giving way to protest. By the end of this decade, dissent was manifest in a body of feminist poetry that articulated the sense of humiliation and deprivation inflicted on womankind by patriarchy and nurtured by women for long — a line of poetry that has developed still further in the eighties.

Nature has inspired Bengali poetry since its origin. Among the post — Tagorean poets Jibanananda Das and Shakti Chattopadhyay have been strongly committed to a Nature that is accessible to the feelings and leads one on an inward journey, a journey from the conscious to the sub-conscious. The majority poets of the sixties had moved away from this feeling for Nature. In the seventies, Nature was back again in the poetic landscape, primarily from the predominance of a generation of poets most of whom had grown up far from the city of Kolkata and had naturally been exposed to Nature in their formative years. The more human habitation turned city-centric, the more it has lost contact with Nature. Nature as subject of treatment yielded place to Man: it is the manners and morals of human life which cornered more and glory in the domain of poetry in preference to the pristine beauty and calm of Nature.

Contrary to the seventies, a predominantly urban spirit highlights the eighties. The city-bred poets face the perils of industrialization.

At almost the same time rank opportunism comes to dominate Indian politics. Money rules supreme in society. People grow to a new realization through various experiences, the frustration of unfulfilled promises, and a sense of mortification. Under the impact of the new socio-political reality, people sought to reasses and redefine their positions at a point outside the maelstrom of change upon change. Mockery came to be the thrust of the poetry of the time. The satiric strain became still sharper.

Yet another striking characteristic of the poetry of the eighties was its development beyond modernism into post-modernism, a convergence of several contradictory directions in both form and content; poetry becoming more an act of construction than composition, intellection ruling over emotion.

But the one subject that has held pride of place in the making of poetry... beyond the mapping offered above... in all these periods has been love. Love as silent prayer; as revelation of hurt, or many a time as dejection. In intense pain or passion or in distant adoration. This everlasting passion continued to fascinate Bengali poets through the vicissitudes of life after Independence, only the expression of the passion varied according to the prevailing idioms of the decade.

Bengali poetry in the last decade of the century again became lyrical; with simple descriptive poems, sometimes more a matter of externals and sometimes more subjective. The turmoil of the outer world has no impact on these poems. The tumults of the surroundings have subsided, political inclinations or values are decided on the rewards they accrue. Personal bitterness, frustration and dejection dominate the poetic language.

As stated earlier, this anthology has endeavoured to document the social, political and socio- economic evolution in the fifty post-Independence years and its impact on Bengali poetry. This is by no means a personal anthology like most other anthologies. The fifty representative poets chosen have won both critical acclaim as well as love and admiration of the readers.

Though the mainstream Bengali poetry has always pivoted in and around Kolkata, we have included poets from North Bengal, Assam and Tripura to give an exhaustive perspective of Bengali poetry and also to highlight the trends of Poetry in these places.

We are quite aware that the original poetry is considerably lost in translation. Especially the nuances are lost in the target language. But left with no other option to take it to a wider section of non-Bengali readers within and outside the country, we have tried not to deviate much from the original. The translators have adhered to the original and have practically taken no liberties. Every poet has an articulation of his/her own, and that is what we have to retain. All measures have been taken by the advisors to ensure this.

Art and poetry are complementary. Poets and painters explore the same imagery. In the Bengali-speaking society, particularly in the period under focus in this book, poets and painters have been in close touch, sharing in common sensibilities and responses. That is yet another dimension of Bengali poetry that we seek to underscore with a selection of representative works projecting the spirit of the times, produced by some of the finest contemporary painters.

The whole project took shape in a span of one and a half years. Kalyani Ghose has coordinated to get the poems translated. She has diligently interacted with the translators throughout the process. We are grateful to her for her participation. Samik Bandopadhyay has found time to advise us on translation, preparing the glossary, and has counselled us from time to time on various aspects of the project. We are indebted to him. Nirmal Kanti Bhattacharjee has been the main inspiring force behind the smooth completion of the project. His confidence in us and his indulgence has escorted us in this long sojourn. We do not have adequate words to record our gratitude. Bengali poetry will remain obliged to him forever. We are also indebted to Sunil Gangopadhyay for being with us throughout this project, critically advising us from time to time to keep us on the right track. Jogen Chowdhury has coordinated and acted as bridge between the artists and us. We are grateful to have him by our side. We are also thankful to the painters for contributing to the shaping of this collection by allowing us to include reproduction of their works. We are also thankful to the translators who have taken time out from their busy schedule to go through the rigours and bring perfection in translating the poems. Finally, we must mention G. K. Jha who has been the main pillar of support for us. We are also thankful to Deb Kumar Basu, secretary P.E.N. West Bengal, for rendering support all through.

But the real credit for making this anthology what it is must go to Barnali Roy who has managed the administration with her customary thoroughness, and her vigilance has extended to all aspect of the project so that she has been, in effect, a co-editor.

We sincerely hope this anthology will find its niche outside Bengal as an exhaustive, reliable and critically invaluable piece of documentation of fifty years of post-colonial Bengali poetry.

Prabal Kumar Basu
Kolkata, October 2001

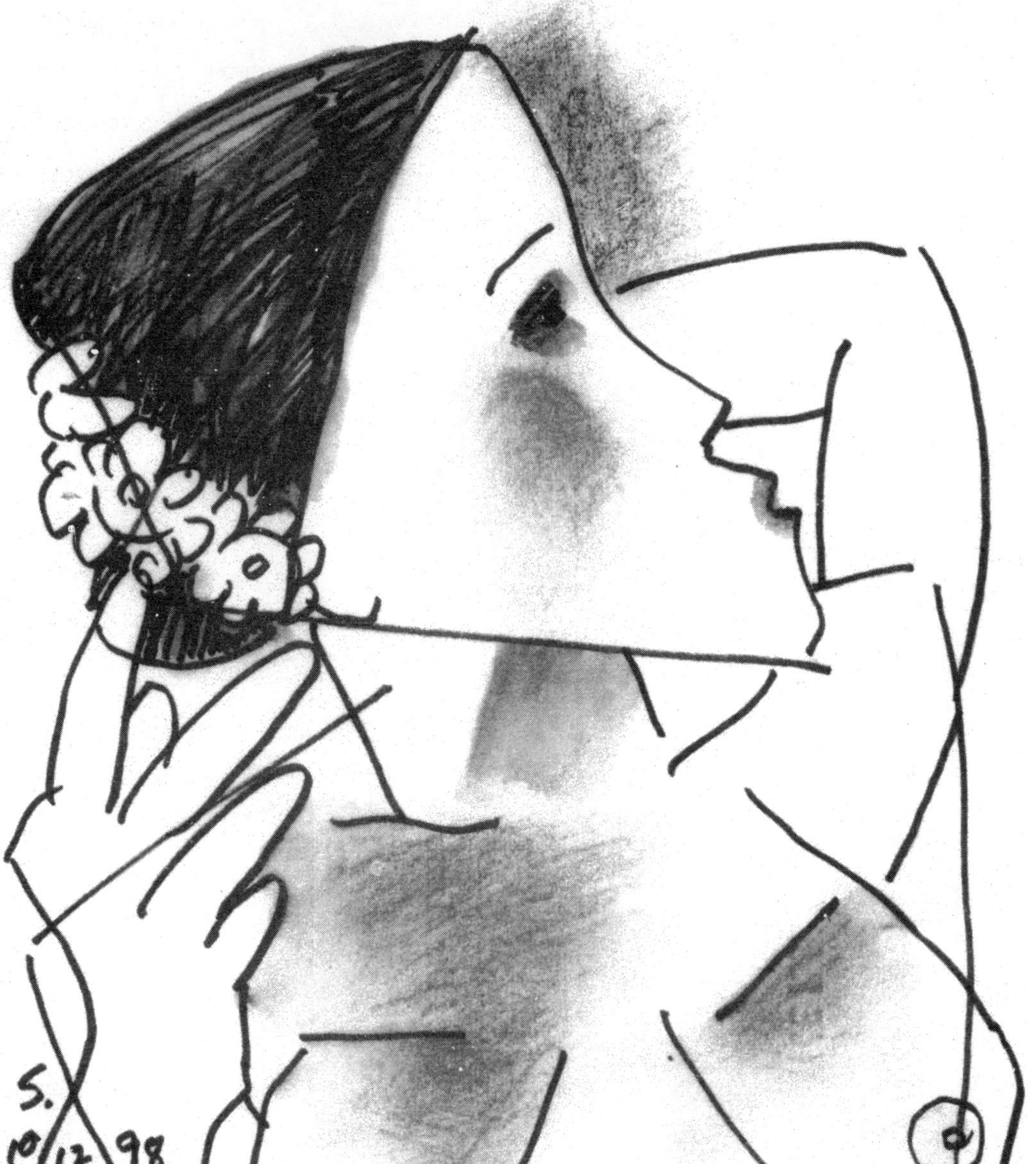
S.
10.12.98

At The Sight Of The Smoke

Arun Mitra

At the sight of the smoke, I knew I had come among humanity, humanity, wandering far and wide with a mad yearning through the thin air in which words did not flow and I could only take a deep breath and hold it back till the lungs came to bursting point and only then I would release my words that would fasten to my chest with sorrow and joy in perfect balance. There was nothing else I could do but search through them in my chest. As I sensed the warmth and saw the dark coils, I burst into joy at the thought that those granules of sorrow and joy would now simmer to the clamour of our frying pans, our spuds, and cooking pots, with all of us together. Look out, it's neither living nor death. Look at all of us, I can hear you, listen to me, I have an endless tale to tell you. Once I have reached finally, let's look out for the one who lights a strong enough fire with a rush of smoke and the houses blazing, bringing down the roofs and the fences dozing close to the earth, in a stifling air, and a heat that does not let me come any closer, How can I look for anyone, and where? I turn away once again. I had a lot to say.

Translation by Samik Bandopadhyay

These Few Lines

Arun Mitra

These few lines are for friends. All that I would like to say is that I am dying to see them once again. When the wind laden with dust wails, my heart twists and turns with it backwards and forwards. I try to identify the routes by which they came, and the direction I've taken. Once the houses crumble on the road, and the numbers get all jumbled, is there any way to learn anything? It's just piles and piles of houses all around. Where's the beam of light emerging through them to help recognition? Lighting a lantern is no use, for it only lets my shadowy arms embrace the whole of the darkness. But then? Then it's only senseless blood, mumbling of the blood: love, dreams, joy etceteras, heaven on earth etceteras. Night perhaps gathers like this. And I hold my breath from time to time craving to catch some scream from afar, just a single one, a single sound stretched along: aw... Hoping it comes towards me, and goes back from me. Futile.

Then is the question no longer one of choosing the direction? For the journey from one birth to yet another?

Translation by Samik Bandopadhyay

The One Who's Come

Arun Mitra

The one who's come is only too familiar,
And yet he remains so indistinct all over
But I've no trace of blindness,
I can rub my eyes and on the street I see
Yet another sparkling day,
The leaves play out against the wind
A game of fox and geese
The roots have sucked up all the sweat and the swoons,
The green flashes with the sheen of sharp edges
That threaten to tear the sky apart
Or drench with blood the hand that dares to touch
Through the open doorway, I can see
Strong beams playing between the ribs of children,
A few torn paper bags on the dust
Simmer in the flames bursting from the eyes.
Yet the one who came to my desolate room
Remains so shadowy.
Did he then come without stepping on the earth?
Had he then never looked at men?

Translation by Samik Bandopadhyay

The Man Never Found Out

Subhas Mukhopadhyay

Alas the man wasted all his life
Trying to safeguard his breast- pocket.

Though,
Had he extended his hand only a little lower down,
He would have discovered Aladdin's wonderful lamp,
His heart.

The man never found out.

His money tree produced money,
Lakshmi came on her stilts,
The walls stood guard so that
Ill-bred air couldn't get in.

Then
as he was busy gobbling up food,
His life slipped out through his fingers —

The man never found out.

Translation by Dr. Partha Ghose

I Am Miserable

Subhas Mukhopadhyay

I am miserable,
        miserable,
                miserable —-
Not because
People are still dying
Like flies in the war of independence
After no less than two world wars.

I am miserable,
        miserable,
                miserable —-

Not because the pack of devilish barbarians
Have discarded their civilised masks
And are beating the beasts hollow in their ferociousness

I am miserable
        miserable
                miserable —-

Only because
Human beings,
Or die-hard born-again human beings?
Capable of tearing apart the flesh and bones of demons,
Are transfixed and silently watching
The fight between Rama and Lakshmana.

I am miserable
> miserable
>> miserable—-

When I find
We have our hand extended towards America
But are calling Vietnam our brother.

Translation by Dr. Partha Ghose

The Knight Check

Subhas Mukhopadhyay

It's not easy to kill my chessmen
One is supported by the other

The knights are playing like hell

Better guard your kings
Or else,
They will be mated by this very check.

The knights are playing like hell.

       2

Boiling oil
Is bubbling over
In the desert's cauldron.

Flee.

Rubber forests
Are thick with hanging nooses.

Flee.

Shoes studded with spikes of greed
Are getting into each other's way
And falling apart.

No taking back your moves,
The whole world is at stake in our game

Tell them,
No matter how they place their pieces,
I am going to take them with my knights.

The knights are playing like hell.

Translation by Dr. Partha Ghose

My Work

Subhas Mukhopadhyay

I want the words to stand on their ownfeet.
I want every shadow to acquire vision.
I want to make still pictures move.

I don't want anybody to call me a poet.
I wish I can keep walking, shoulder to shoulder,
Until the very last day of my life.

I wish I could lay down my pen
By the tractor and say,
Let me call it a day, brother,
Pass me the fire.

Translation by Dr. Partha Ghose

To Hangers On

Subhas Mukhopadhyay

I know, every time I sit down to play chess
A hundred thousand hangers-on
Would rush and fall over my shoulders.
They would abandon their work
And wish to guide me on every move
Of mine, as if I were a parrot.

I wonder if I should tell them now
with folded hands——
Gentlemen,
Either sit down quietly and watch
Or go back to your own places.

For heavens sake,
Let me play my own game.

Translation by Dr. Partha Ghose

In The Meeting Of Poets

Birendra Chattopadhyay

As long as there was light
One could make out the faces, as long as
Darkness was not so terribly
Intense.

Or masks, I saw only masks
In the light at the meeting. As it darkened,
Everyone shredded their disguise
And went home, to security.
I am left alone, innocent boy.

Translation by Kalyani Ghose

The Amazing Smell Of Rice In The Night Sky

Birendra Chattopadhyay

An old fairy tale

A girl is lying on her face and sobbing in agony
Her eyes are pale, but very sweet.
A boy does not know that, so he sleeps soundly
Had he known, he would have been on Pegasus.

Translation by Kalyani Ghose

Behula's Raft

Birendra Chattopadhyay

On the river Gangur floats Behula's raft,
Looking at it, empty hearted, I lie awake all night —
My motherland plays with paper boats.

Translation by Kalyani Ghose

Headless Trunks Scream In Glee

Birendra Chattopadhaya

The earth is filled with the mercy of God

Endless in this mercy,
That place of execution that we call our motherland
The executioner lavishes love on the babe at arms, his sport?
The poets compose poems, patriotism deepens gradually, hemorrhage in the womb
The headless trunk shout in glee, the colourful, the colourful,
What game are you playing? The earth bends like a bow in pain
In the bazaar, the great leader hawks Karl Marx, Lenin, Stalin, Gandhi
For a paisa each.

Translation by Kalyani Ghose

Naren Master

Arun Sarkar

Spelling, pronunciation, meaning and use
You, taught me all wrong, master !
When I speak out, clever people burst into laughter,
The fools look on vacant,
And the hefty guys with rolled up sleeves, say;
Push this fellow out by the neck.

In your hopeless effort to turn jackals and donkeys into men
You became hard and tolerant like a column.
I don't have that patience, master, not that strength in the spine.
Blow after blow and block after block
Have turned me dumb and desolate.
You taught me all wrong, master all wrong.
I have now rolled up my reel,
I don't venture into the crowd, don't peep into neighbour's houses
I talk with myself alone.

Yet when the local urchins
Lift my blinds, make faces at me and enquire,
Where were you taught, grandpa?
I don't keep mum at all,
I declare puffing out my chest:
Why, at the school of Naren master.

Translation by Kalyan Dasgupta

Destitute

Arun Sarkar

The tree belongs to me yet the flowers bloom at will.
Or is it season's frolic? I can't think any more.
Is there anybody free on earth? Am I myself free?
As ever such queer thoughts confuse me
Once I went to yield myself to you
But taking three steps back I ran
And then could regain my breath.
If I come to you again would you take me in?
How alone I'm left today, bankrupt without succour

Translation by Kalyan Dasgupta

Father

Arun Sarkar

My father died at fifty-one
I'm now older than my father.
Touching fifty-four my hair is almost grey.
Withdrawn and somewhat coward
My movements to and fro are bound
In this small cabin here.

But when I think of father
I turn at once a lad
Clad in torn shrts, reel in hand
Nineteen thirty-five rolls back.
I fly the entire sky
But it's not easy at all to reach my father.

Translation by Kalyan Dasgupta

A Summer Poem

Arun Sarkar

You I desire, you alone
No peace for me without you.
Ignite my summer nights days and
With the rakta kingshuk.

The ocean burns in ecstasy
The phosphorus coiled round its body
Let your hair flow in the darkness
Let the nails strike your white chest blue.

You I desire, you alone
The horses' hooves beat in desperation
Lightning flashes at every footstep
A shrill scream bursts forth.

I can't let you go, no peace without you
I've touched the rose enough;
Ignite my summer nights days and
With the rakta kingshuk.

Translation by Kalyan Dasgupta

All Kinds Of Loving

Nirendranath Chakrabarty

There are times when I feel
May be all life's journeys
Are near ending. But
Just then
Before my eyes there opens out
The dusty road
My feet have never trod.

There are times when I feel
I've resolved all the bother of loving,
 But just then erupts
A sudden heart-wrenching
Feeling of letdown.

How can I speak of those
I do not know? But
Even those I did know remain
Unspoken of;
Beset by this midnight thought
I get out of bed
And step out to the balcony.

I see the city below
Like a half-sunken ship
Drowning deeper still
In sleep, while
The darkling trees stand still.

Yet just then
A tempest rages through the sky
Setting myriad stars ashiver.

On a street in Calcutta
I had once seen
A naked boy who's cherubic face
Drifts across the monsoon sky
And floats before my eye.

Translation by Madhuchhanda Karlekar

The Palace

Nirendranath Chakrabarty

Once, as a boy
I had slipped into
A derelict, moss-laden palace.
How many wings, how many chambers,
Hidden cubicles
And courtyards and
Stairways, and
Verandahs it had
Though I wandered all afternoon
As one possessed
I still could not tell.

When I think of Rabindranath
I am reminded
Of that wondrous palace.
Except this one
Is not derelict, nor mossy;
A vast, unending edifice
We can still explore
With curious minds and
Awe-struck eyes
Explore for ages.

Translation by Madhuchhanda Karlekar

It's So At Times

Nirendranath Chakrabarty

There are those days when right from the morning
I feel my heart
Turn somersaults inside.
I feel somehow different.
The sky looks
A shade bluer than usual,
The greenery all around
A shade greener.

I want to smile and talk with my neighbours.
Even approach strangers
And befriend them too.
Call out to one and all
At the Shyambazar crossing: How are you?

Not every day, but
Once in a while it's so.
Then I kick aside banana skins
from the middle of the road.
If I see someone leaning too far over a parapet
I scream: Watch out!

Translation by Madhuchhanda Karlekar

Seeing It Through To The End

Nirendranath Chakrabarty

Getting in was none too easy.
But surprisingly,
Two or three stations later
The compartment was near empty.

So long
I hardly had room to place a foot.
Now
I quickly spread out my dhurrie.
Next
I placed my suitcase on a bunk,
My water pitcher under a bench,
And sat back relaxed.
Just then
A callow sort of checker came along.
He winked and said,
What's the point, old pal,
You'll be off at the next station,
So why stretch out so comfortably,
What's the use?

I said, Hell,
I'm going somewhere else,
Why should I
Hop off midway just like that?
He smiled and said,
Well, I don't know, but many do.

I didn't smile.
I put my feet up,
Settled in snugly saying,
Many have no hair on their lip
Even at thirty-five,
So leave them aside.

Checker says, So you're not getting off ?

Without wasting words
I undid my dhoti–knot,
Took my yellow ticket out
And waved it in front of his nose,
Let others get off,
I, Sir, will not,
Now that I've found a place,
I'll see this through to the end.

Translation by Madhuchhanda Karlekar

Jesus Of Calcutta

Nirendranath Chakrabarty

No red signal glared warning,
Yet the tempest-rush of Calcutta city
Came to a sudden halt;
All traffic lurched precariously,
Taxicabs private cars tempo vans,
And tiger-brand double-deckers
Stood stock-still.
Those who hollered   Watch out!
As they rushed to the kerb in alarm
Head-loaders, vendors, shopkeepers, customers
Now stand like frozen figures
On an artist's easel.
Dumb-struck they watch
Proceeding across the road
With small faltering feet
A stark naked child.

The rain stopped a short while ago
Here on Chowringhee.
Now the sun has appeared again
Piercing the heart of the clouds
With a lengthened shaft;
The city is bathed in an enchanting light.

I look out of the state bus window
Gaze once at the sky, then down on you.
Child of a beggar-woman
Jesus of Calcutta,

You have stopped all traffic by your spell.

Stricken cries, surly drivers ' gnashing teeth,
Yet you remain oblivious.
As Death looms large on either hand,
You go tottering on.
The quintessence of humanity, celebrating
Your newly -acquired pace, eager
To grasp the whole world
In your fist. And so
With faltering steps
You traverse the earth from end to end.

Translation by Madhuchhanda Karlekar

Ashtray

Manindra Gupta

In the last visit to my family doctor, I found
On his table a human heart of regular size
Who knows what it was made of, it looked like a fresh heart —-
As if it had just then been wrenched out of a patient's breast
I wondered what the doctor's thoughts were as he
Pressed the stetho a few times on the chest, then looked absently
At the heart on the table, and gently said
May I take a cardiograph ?

A hundred rupees down the drain! But I could not demur – as if
The heart on the table was mine. Any disobedience
Would make the doctor wind it up tightly enough to break its spring
After the electrocardiogram, the doctor said
Continue the same medicine, the same dose. Come again after six months
I tried to say ... the medicines cost three hundred rupees a month ...
Any alternative ...any change...
The doctor took the heart in his hand like a paperweight
As if he would squeeze it just then. My voice choked –
o.k ...o.k...
Come after seven days to take the cardiogram report
Yes, sir.

Seven days later when I visited his chamber I found the doctor
Cheerfully smoking a cigarette
On the table the two chambers of that fresh-looking heart
Were stuffed with cigarette butts and ash

Translation by Rolla GuhaNeogy

The Pilot

Manindra Gupta

In the rather quiet cockpit the pilot held his coffee and watched
The flying machine of Narada coming towards him.. his wife's lover
Could be seen in the same way approaching
Amidst the sparkling whiteness of the atmosphere
He had just switched on the auto-pilot to relax with his coffee!
No, he would not change direction any more. Better still,
Let their be a stunning crash.
In this monotonous life its quite sometime a gift has been offered to anyone
He waited expectantly in order to see : how the sparks
And molten fire from the mid – air collission below fall
And make up his wife's face

Translation by Rolla GuhaNeogy

The Candle

Manindra Gupta

This candle is a complex plant
Like a widowed mother it wears away
Weeping silently in the kitchen
That noon, when the elder daughter- in- law broke the rice pitcher with a piece of
                                                      firewood
And sat glumly, feet outstretched,
The candle, like the younger daughter-in-law
Flashed a smile that evening
And extinguished in a sudden burst of wind blowing into the bamboo thicket

It has stood for years in churches, flickering
Like the tremulous notes of choral songs,—-
We thought this was its true nature
But the other day during a walk by the riverside
In a moment it transformed into a mirror- eyed fish
And jumped deep into the river!

On this rainy day in this room
The candle cries in the shrill voice of a desperate peacock
That cry like a stream of blood
Sprays the damp wall all around
I too can not restrain myself in my room today–
I shall take the candle into the forest, in twilight hours
Amid the rain- soaked trees
Where, in the dying light can be seen the sign of fire on the crest
                                                  of the shomi tree

The candle is an extraordinary female plant

Translation by Rolla GuhaNeogy

To My Friends' Wives

Sarat Kumar Mukhopadhyay

We were having a great time
Our wrangles shook the railings; our guffaws mirth the footpaths
A host of long familiar faces.
Who are you? Whose virgin maids?
Unseen, you perched lightly upon the wires like a bird
Rubbed your beak in your feathers for a while
And then
Holding a friend's hands flew away to the other side of the road.

See! That leaves just the two of us, old friends still together,
But what can only two talk about?
Under the shadows of the light-post
Two faces look at each other with apprehension
Look up to the electric wires— no birds
Not a single bird on those wires;

Why do you mirthlessly titter from the other side of the road ?

Translation by Sutapa Neogi

Bending Down And Down

Sarat Kumar Mukhopadhyay

Bending down and down, the head has touched the feet
How much more should I bend?
Men stand beside men, yet their shoulders do not touch
           Their hearts do not melt,
O! What a life is this? Take this life back
           And let me return once more
To flow like semen into my old, seminal self, wherein lies
           The dried kernel of untold agonies of a virile, old man.

Or else, I shall grasp your feet together
           And tear out
All the salutations 'neath your ten toe nails,
And forgive me if the head that bows in respect,
 Suddenly recoils, without reason.
Smeared with the ashes of hatred.

Translation by Sutapa Neogi

Sounds

SaratKumar Mukhopadhyay

A fox and a frog peddled the dark late into the night.
While we - each his own - deepened our slumber and our embraces,
They went away.

A pair of crows and a cock
Slid through the windows, surreptitiously,
Like the long neck of a camel;
Pecked furiously at the tiny spheres of the mosquito net
And, polished them off totally!
As I opened my eyes I saw
Hanging on four square pegs,
Another dazzling white day.

Yet sometimes in my slumber
Somewhere, the sound of waters lapping
The sound of steamer hooting—
I don't quite comprehend

Translation by Sutapa Neogi

Birajmohan

SaratKumar Mukhopadhyay

Birajmohun now thinks of the futility of his life.
This July morning, a solemn sky
Yonder the wavering gum tree
A lonely milk van performing the rounds of duty.
Just like a crow caws perfunctorily
Some one in the neighbour hood slum coughs incessantly;
Birajmohan thinks, whatever he could grab, perforce
He has acquired
Whatever he could manipulate dexterously, all of it
Has slowly crept into his reach.
The paddy has been planted in his village fields
The cowshed brimming with milking cows and frolicking calves.

Is this the time for reflection! He wonders
If he has seen it all? Has he scrutinized life well enough?
Does any old wound linger?
Is it necessary to correct any blunder?

Someone in the neighbourhood slum coughs continuously in the morning
Birajmohan for the first time in his life, today
Thinks about its futility.

Translation by Sutapa Neogi

Secret Abode

Aloke Sarkar

I long for a house
Where my lover resides.
Every afternoon I will go to her house
Now, it is afternoon and look how many
Bright and happy faces pass by.
They must be heading to their lover's place
Which way should I go
To locate my lover's abode?
So many windows, so many eyes staring at the road
Bloodless brown, my afternoons are steeped in sadness, even now
They pass by exuding happiness through the lively rhythm of their gait
They must be going where their lovers reside.
They are normal, when will I pick up such a normal rhythm?
Where is the terrace of the house in a lane
With a red sari fluttering in the wind!
Happiness I want and through the whole afternoon.
I will search out a lover's house
Having located their lover's abode
The rhythm of their engrossed walk
Appears to have lit up a continuous stream of illumination.
I too have put on festive
Clothes in my secret room.
Which way to my lover's house?
I too long for a lover's abode
I'll surely wipe out all the darkness.

Translation by Pradip Banerjee

Which Way Is Heaven

Aloke Sarkar

Which way is heaven I wonder
God resides under a fig tree
Next to that market place
Every one accepts money with open palms
Me too, as if I was a blind man
Unwavering melody of melancholy
 I decided to ask a far away friend, but
Feel scared by a barrier of formal faces
But I am sure there is someone who'd answer everything
In a flash.

White clouds roam in the sky of my room
How to go to that person!
For a calm and clear hearing
Misguided dust glides over the field
As if from the earlier birth
Where would I lose myself?
I haven't spent a penny
Night with accumulated wealth
Hard desires
Light in exchange of what?
Sympathetic yet severe divide.

It happens in a flash
Why wouldn't there be a
Dense morning that can
Take me to Heaven?

Flowers, fruits, engrossed hours in prayer
Or two hands held in love
I look at the dull moonlight
Pale and worn out, resonance inside
A sick candle burns on the wall
The candle burns
Its light, scared and brown.

Translation by Pradip Banerjee

Every Day He Watches

Aloke Sarkar

Today he looked differently
An eagle sitting on the top
Of the coconut tree
When it flew away
The leaves were shivering.

The very old, tottering coconut tree
Courtyard of a bygone era
Cluster of glum moss on the wall
Every day he watches
Today he looked differently
A rat ran away alongside the well.

The house dating back
To grandfather's time
The cornice dilapidated
A corner of the roof has crumbled
Entering the room he found
A gleam of light has sneaked in through the window
A very soft gleam of light.

And then he felt scared
For the first time he felt
Such an old house
Shattering the silence
His son runs down

The staircase
Silent sparrows keep on
Chirping in the hall below.

Translation by Pradip Banerjee

See

Aloke Sarkar

You are my friend
Seeing you after ages
Come inside my house and
Into my room
See how I have decked up my
Study table
Bought a painting in red
Hung it up on the eastern wall
Do come in
Red carpet on the staircase
The glass doors are glistening
Open the door and come in
See my face, eyes, health
All full of brightness
Wearing a new style shirt
Open the door and come
There will not be any sound
Go straight towards south
There will not be any sound
Sit on the soft mattress
As if you are sinking
No sound whatsoever
The flower vase in glowing blue
Roses tied in a string
A room steeped in light and darkness
All windows and doors closed

It is not at all hot, not cool either
There is no breeze to
Dishevel your hair, neither
Will papers fly
The roses will not sway or bend
Sit inside the room, do sit
There will not be any sound
Do recline a bit when you sit
Throw your shoes at the corner
No sound either
You are my old friend
Seeing you after ages
Can you hear me?
There is no sound anywhere
Your hair is not getting disheveled
By the breeze
The bunch of roses does not bend or sway
You are my old friend
See my room
The bunch of roses neither bend nor
Sway.

Translation by Pradip Banerjee

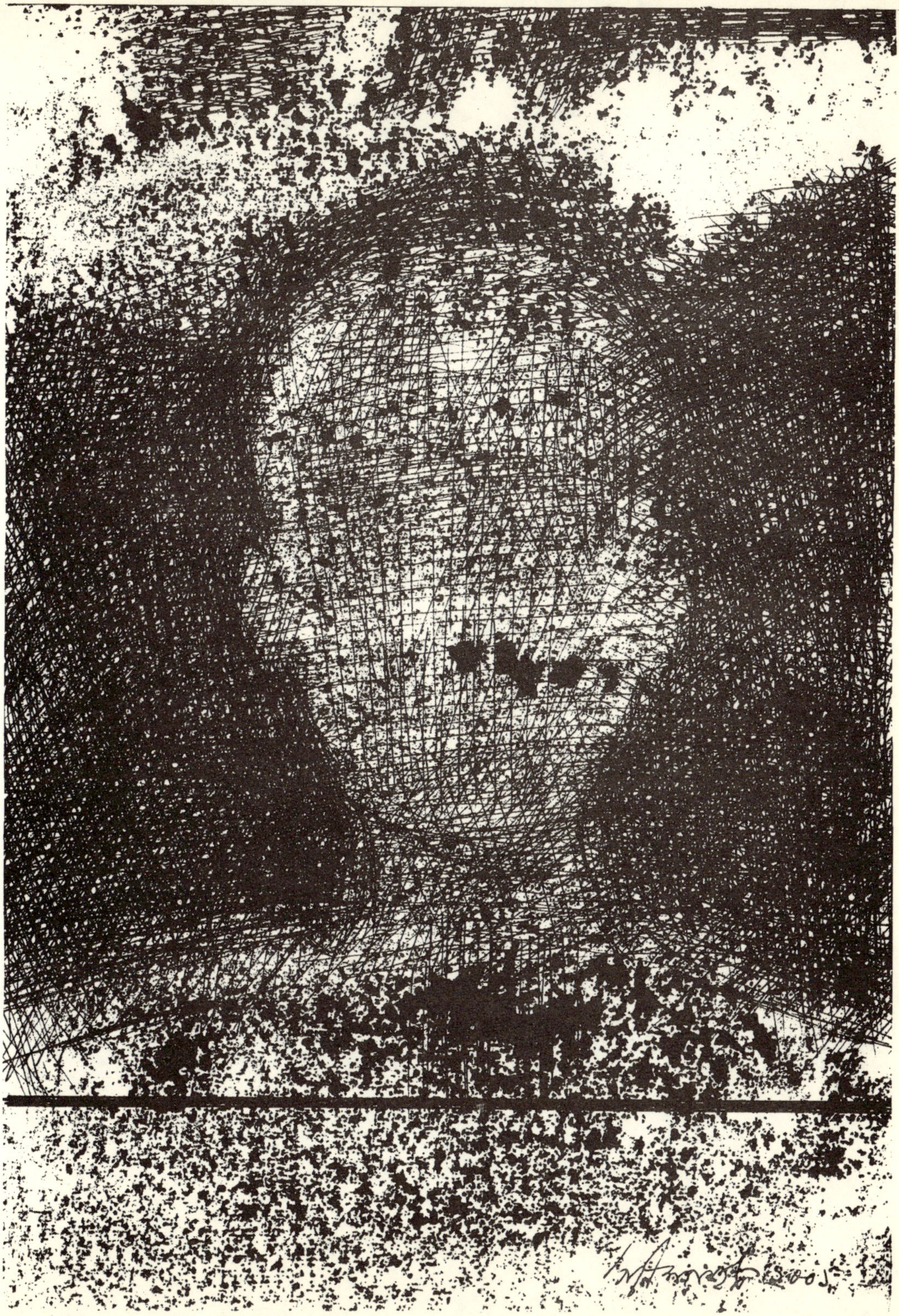

The Babu Says

Shankha Ghosh

I go on talking
And reading books
Living life?
Leave that to the menials

Those who are dying
Let them die for their own fault !
With my brains, I know,
I am the brightest of all

Though I spurn human touch
My heart and brain lie bound
In the knowledge of humanity
I can change the world
In theory and discourse
Living life ?
Let that be for the menials

Even if they say
I am false and sham
Even when the fire of my words
Set my own home ablaze
While being burnt
I look through the window
And find all those menials
Living life !

Translation by Bandana Sanyal

Beautiful

Shankha Ghosh

One has to go somewhere, so I come
Its just that and nothing more
The drowned shadow of the deep filled the end of the sky

One has to see something, so I see
The end of the cornfields
The saffron bosom of the water
The villages lose themselves in one another
Only the twelfth night wakes

Its my nature to get lost
So I have lost my way
But I know, I remember
Who tricked me here

The rocky motionlessness
There was no conversation around
In secret I myself had drowned her
Faking fishing in the desolate santhali lake
No, none aimed his arrow at me
I am saved ! what an escape!

The shadow of the deep fills the horizon
They know nothing,
Let them know, rid my sin
The blue stream races

The deep gorge fills with compassion
If all on a sudden
His own shadow embraces him and says:
'Aren't you beautiful? Why do you exist at all?'

Translation by Bandana Sanyal

A Big Fool, Unsocial Too

Shankha Ghosh

On returning home do you feel you talked too much?
Artfulness, do you feel much tired?

Feel like lighting an incense stick
And sit in silence, after a bath
In your blue chamber?

Feel like doing off the demonic garb
And wear your human body for once?

As melting time streams through your room
Do you feel happy
Stretching on a floating raft in everlasting sleep

If that is so, come back. Adieu, artfulness

They will call you a big fool,
They will call you an unsocial, too !

But does it matter?

Translation by Bandana Sanyal

Idle Water

Shankha Ghosh

Feet-deep idle water, do you remember me?
I left you as darkness fell
Like the aerial roots of a tree reaching the earth

I don't exactly remember
How much of the sky and wind of Bengal was real
And how much my own creation

The blueness of a forehead in such collyrium - darkness
The emptiness woven in dense locks
Flanging like trees all around

But.. where did I really go? Boatman
The rippling sound of my Bengal faded far away

That magic sound, yearning for the boat, airborne evening prayers
You've not handed me anything, just sent me off

It is my memory that is my city, my playful unsure hands
Why did I fail to bear you in my heart, that night?

Translation by Bandana Sanyal

The Decade

Shankha Ghosh

Three white haired women asked one another
In the manner of olden days:
Why is it so quiet all around?
Where are those young men?

The afternoon glow fades out
The debt of the martyrs' monument
Dissolves in hushed breath
Yet another day passes by

Between the monument and the old women
Some bones have turned to grass
They jab the feet once they catch someone alone
To ask: Do you hear anything at all?

The debt of the decade stalks out there
With a garland of heads about its neck
The old women call out: Smart young men
Don't you have anything to say?

Translation by Barnali Roy

The Blood Stained Lattice Window

Alokeranjan Dasgupta

The two of them had come for a walk in the paddy field
The two of them are on the run, leaving a child in the paddy field

' To the station now,' said one of them
' To the station now,' said the other

' Come down the bridge,' said one to the other
' Come down the bridge,' said one to the other

And then they came down to see the paddy boat sailing away
With the bloodstained child lying on a beautiful quilt

Translation by Samik Bandopadhyay

The Late Afternoon Sky

Alokeranjan Dasgupta

From within the abandoned water pipe
A bird weaves its pattern of notes

A large sick family, living off the call girl
Has shaken up her makeup

The villains have hurled a dynamite at the Red Cross van
Killing three more children, the numbers of no account any more

Who were those who sparked off a civil war, and then with innocent faces
Carried off the woman in the second stanza of this poem
To Diamond Harbour for a picnic?

The late afternoon sky broods over my cowardice

Translation by Samik Bandopadhyay

The Evening Press Conference

Alokeranjan Dasgupta

The General is in the best of spirits today
Pointing to the Medallion for Heroism on the chest of his khaki uniform
He told us: ' The war's in fine shape today, its stomach
Bursting with riches.' A Jordanian reporter asked:' How many enemies killed?'
The General took umbrage:' We don't have time to count the dead.
The war's in fine shape today, feeling fresh and sprightly
The orchard of weaponry is quite intact
Even after the annihilation of the bastards
The war's in fine shape today, and with that the press conference is over
With thanks to all of you. Mind you don't miss
The cocktails arranged by courtesy of the war.'

Translation by Samik Bandopadhyay

Roads Lost In Temples And Mosques

Alokeranjan Dasgupta

The woman custom's officer
At the airport at Ukrainia
Exclaimed "What a mess! It's a visa for Russia!"

In Russia, at the word
Leningrad, uttered by mistake
They ordered us to leave

On our way back
We found all those lands where we had indulged in fun
On our way up, had split into segments

Throughout the return journey
We wonder: Maybe we don't have visas any longer
For where we had set out at the start!

Translation by Samik Bandopadhyay

Jarasandha

Shakti Chattopadhyay

Why did you bring me forth, take me back.

I ask you to use your motherly hands to take back the face that is cold as darkness, the eyes that are stingy, as the dried up lake. No more this field, the feet are sore with the piercing paddy stubble. Why did you bring me here, trampling, trampling and trampling over the body of plain vegetables, take me back.

The smell of rotten paddy, of moss, of the scales of three-eyed fish in shallow water, all these have become rows of your spice jars in my dark chamber of feelings, mother. When I cannot see the hands or feet of dismembered darkness, where have you brought me, leaning on your decrepitude? I can never see the hands and feet of dismembered darkness.

A soft breeze makes me feel the sea is near. Your firm arms, Jara, hold me back. The implication - if I take a dip with all the darkness of everything I have, the sea will recede, cold will recede, death will recede.

Maybe, you gave birth to death rather than life. I am darkness, I will remain darkness or will be darkness.

Why did you bring me forth, take me back.

Translation by Dr. Partha Ghose

Pleading Portrait

Shakti Chattopadhyay

When it's time to part
Tell me how it came about
How that you want to flee me?
A road-side pebble you might get
You wretched girl
Love's trembling blossom I didn't have
What could I offer you?
Look, the garden is all bare
To Roro's banks I will take you
I strove to blot out everyone's gloom
When I saw you
But time, my time ran out

Never ever will I come back again
To get over my frustration with you
Everyone used to say
Come back when you wish
On such and such a month
Ten times a year!
You said to me
Don't bother to come
Wasting time lifelong for work.

Translation by Dr. Partha Ghose

Unruly I Roam

Shakti Chattopadhyay

What furious uproar on the shore
'Whose corpse is floating by
Where was his home?'
The night's babble would only iterate
'Unruly I roam'.

Is the ocean equally welcome
To the dead and the living
In so completely unguarded an instant?
Who knows if venom is the right drink
Nectar is poison indeed!
Fatigue grows in the brain incessant.

What furious uproar on the shore
'Whose corpse is floating by
Where was his home?'
The night's babble would only iterate
'Unruly I roam'.

Translation by Dr. Partha Ghose

O Forever Venerable Fire

Shakti Chattopadhyay

O forever venerable fire
Burn me.
First burn those two legs
That are unable to move any more,
Then the arms that have neither love
Nor any neatness left in them today.
Ice cold flowers lie trapped by the arms now
No responsibility rests on the shoulders any more
Go burn them at life's altar
Tarry a little, then destroy
The seat of knowledge
Silenced of truth and falsehood, colour and its absence
Save the two eyes,
Perhaps there are still things for them to see
Destroy the eyes after the tears have run dry
Don't burn the garlands and bouquets
Tousled with fragrance
The touch of loving hands still lingers on them.
Let him float by along the Ganges, wayward, free ...
O forever venerable fire
Burn me.

Translation by Dr. Partha Ghose

That isn't Time For Much Joy –
That Isn't Time For Much Happiness

Shakti Chattopadhyay

Legs right up to the head wobble, wall after wall, cornice to cornice,
                footpaths swap at midnight
While going home, home within home, leg within leg,
                chest within chest
Nothing else (a lot more?) – even before that
Legs right up to the head wobble, wall after wall, cornice to cornice,
                footpaths swap at midnight
While going home, home within home, leg within leg,
                chest within chest
Nothing else.
'Hands up' – keep your hands raised – until someone picks you up and
Carries you away
Black car again within black car, within it yet another
Black car
Rows of windows, doors, graveyards, - skeletons helter-skelter
White termites within skeletons, life within termites, death within
Life – therefore
Death within death
Nothing else
'Hands up' – keep your hands raised – until someone picks you up and
Carries you away
Picks you up and flings you out of the car, but into another one
In which someone always awaits you – like banyan saplings clinging on
To wall plaster
Someone or the other, whom you don't know
Awaits you under cover of leaves like a tough bud

A golden spider-web noose in hand –
To garland you – your wedding is at midnight when footpaths swap
                                        legs right up to the head wobble
Wall after wall, cornice to cornice.
Imagine stations running leaving the trains behind, starlight next to a
                                                              dim bulb
Imagine, shoes walking, legs motionless – heaven and earth
                                         topsy-turvy
Imagine, palanquins carrying the dead running towards Nimtala
On the shoulders of children –
In the world beyond
The old engaged in vertical bridal-chamber dance
That isn't time for much joy – which isn't time for much happiness
Right then
Legs right up to the head wobble, wall after wall, cornice to cornice,
                      footpaths swap at midnight
While going home, home within home, leg within leg,
                      chest within chest
Nothing else.

Translation by Dr. Partha Ghose

Nineteen Seventy One

Sunil Gangopadhyay

O mother, your teenage daughter has disappeared forever
Mother, the younger brother next to me is also no more
I last saw him in terrible November
When he ran past me in the dark, with a rifle in his hand..

Today there is celebration all around, waves of victorious joy break over us
Mother's dry eyes remember her missing daughter and moisten
Her hands are outstretched, if they hold a mirror
I am also busy searching the fields for the corpse of my younger brother

Those who go they go, those who are left behind know the pain of loneliness
Ajiur, Ajijur, I had promised you my yellow shirt
Why didn't you take a whiff of my body's breath before you left for heaven?

A tall thin boy with a whip-like body, in the chin
Scar of a childhood cut, still a child in the eyes of the mother
Always stubborn and head strong, would bring from
The deep core of river's bed handfulls of mud to win a bet
How do I recognise him now light under torch in rotten debris

O mother, I last saw your daughter Lavanya on the 3rd of July
Chased by soldiers, she plunged into the raging waters of the monsoon river
Hauled up in a net she was struggling to free herself, a captured mermaid
Then I was chained to a post on the river bank jetty

The animals dragged her away, suddenly Lavanya turned and
Stared at everyone's eyes, her look was like thunder
A chit of a girl got transformed in a moment into a mother-goddess

Even the river was not spared from the curse of the sacred virgin
Mother, I have looked for your Lavanya everywhere, in the bunkers, in foxholes
Wherever I have spotted a piece of torn woman's clothing drenched in blood
Tell — tale signs of ravished chastity
Over the hundreds of Ajiur, their white bones pierce the darkness
Somewhere a hand clawed into earth for support

Those who go they go, those who remain learn to smile
Rubbing the tears with the back of the left hand
Flower-thief stealthily enters the grave
I wake up at midnight
Children clap in their play and birds start returning to the nest

Translation by Sreemati Mukherjee

A City Of Memories

Sunil Gangopadhyay

I hold in my hands the first book of poems by a callow youth
Its jacket, not so skillfully designed smells of greenness
Its pages, light as butterflies
Are covered with moving letters
The titles seek to fly off, the words eager to
Change places.

The young man waits, his face conveys
Doubt, conflict, pride, embarrassment
And defiance.
He does not speak, his silence strikingly vocal.
I cannot fathom what he thinks of me
But in him, I can identify myself exactly as I am
I sneak a look at him. Searching for the
Tear at the side of the collar.

Hands in his pocket
He must be counting the loose change
I feel an urge to change places with him
                Straightaway.

Translation by Barnali Roy

For Che Guevera

Sunil Gangopadhyay

Che, your death makes me feel guilty
My lips dry up, my chest feels empty
My soul hears the incessant rainfall
A mournful sigh from the childhood
Che, your death makes me feel guilty.

In the jungles of Bolivia, your blue pantaloon clad
Mutilated body
A dried line of blood down your bare chest
The gaping eyes
That gaze roves from one hemisphere to the other
Che, your death makes me feel guilty.

I look back in retrospect from my childhood to youth
I was also supposed to be by your side, armed
I was also supposed to toil in the jungles, in mud, and hide in stone caves
Preparing for the right moment of revolt
I was also supposed to run with the heavy rifle butt on my shoulders
Unleashing a war cry
I was also supposed to sing the freedom song
Amidst the hot pool of blood and lacerated bodies
But I'm constantly getting late.

So long I was alone; I've endured insults
                with my head down
But I did not accept defeat, I did not compromise
I repeated my promise sitting by the train window
Walking by the desolate river bank

On the lonely alley of the field
At the burning ghat
I had promised the sky, the rains the trees,
               the sudden dust storms
 I was getting ready to avenge everything
                in my own way
I would make a comeback
I clenched my fists, tightened my jaws
 I repeated many a time to myself
My vow to fight back
Che, your death makes me feel guilty

I'm still not prepared; I'm constantly getting late
I'm still in the tunnel, in the zone of light — and-shade
I'm getting delayed
Che, your death makes me feel guilty.

Translation by Barnali Roy

Neera's Illness

Sunil Gangopadhyay

Kolkata is plunged into misery when Neera is unwell
When the sun dies down, the neons before bursting out in light find out
           Is Neera well today?
The old clock at the church, the shops red in glory, they know
           Neera is doing fine today
Lakhs of people at the office, cinema, park
           Spread Neera's news
The strong fragrance of Bokul carries the happiness of Neera
Suddenly a wayward drift chiming a berserk note
Playfully crisscrosses the sky
Everyone in Kolkata with a knowing smile on their lips
Learn Neera has gone for a walk today.

When the sky is covered with clouds, the city is down cast
           Stifled with gloom
Suddenly a taxi runs into the belly of a tram
Creating a depressing jam in the crossing
Dejected faces line the restaurant, the roads
           Disgusted facades.
Entire Kolkata is outraged and in strike, creates havoc
Burning telephone poles, postoffice
The beating hearts of every individual too declare a strike
I shiver in fear. I know, I instantly run to her and cry out
           Neera are you sad?
My sweet girl, please open your eyes once, show me your loving face
           As seen in mirror
Singing like the rippling waters, please answer the riddle!
At once the cloud is lifted, it rains

Heaving a sigh of relief, people depart
To watch a movie or a match.

The knots of traffic jam loosen, the cycle and tempo
The car and the rickshaw find the ways to their destinations in harmony
Cigarette hanging from his lips, someone says
It is not too bad to be alive.

Translation by Barnali Roy

The Nurse-Maid

Sunil Gangopadhyay

My nursemaid is sitting on the footpath of Sealdah
With both palms outstretched
Her lips are quivering from time to time
All will think she's a blind old riff raff refugee lady

She had once picked me up from my dying mother's arms
In the labour room
And given me shelter in her bosom
I had sucked her youthful breasts
Everyday drank her blood
I had howled crouched in her intimate smelling breast
Sitting with her legs outstretched in the sun
She used to mollycoddle and massage me

So many a times I heard from my mother aunts
How she had bathed at a new moon midnight
To bring me medicinal herbs
When I had cholera
She had promised an Amlaki at the darga of Satyapir
        For my cure.

The old rag was begging for a two-paisa coin
I searched my pocket for ten paise
To replace the quarter my hand felt

My dear nursemaid, you had given light to my eyes
Opened them and had poured rose water
You had thrown open the world before me.

But which world have you introduced me to?
You old wretch, why did you let me live
In this unbelievable world
What more will I have to sacrifice?

Translation by Barnali Roy

Me and My Oleander Flower

Benoy Mazumdar

At the end of the day's work blessed sleep comes
Like a shadow and spreads its shades
We lie in close embrace me and my Oleander Flower
Across the sky light and darkness are wrapped together in different ways
All the stars mingle their light
Craving for love, chaste in their desire
When work is done, blessed sleep treads like a shadow to give refuge
We lie in each other's arms, me and my Oleander Flower

Translation by Deepa Mukhopadhyay

Can Give You Love

Benoy Mazumdar

I can give you love, can you receive it ?
All things are scattered away from your playful palms —
Laughter, moonlight, pain, memory, nothing remains
This is my realisation. The pigeons don't ever
Unfurl its wings by moonlight; but I can still give you my love
This is my truest and easiest gift — let not the seed
Face any obstacle in sprouting green
Let it not turn pale and yellow, crushed in darkness
And yet, what pain makes me hold on to the chilly stone
                of death, lest I love someone
It is you who are not able to take my love ! You pigeon, you remain
Unhurt even when you fall from your perch on the tree, you
                still fly away
And you –you will leave, with the everlasting smiles
As seen in the old paintings; I will remain stilled in the pain of my wound!

Translation by Deepa Mukhopadhyay

Last Evening

Benoy Mazumdar

Last evening a farmer came and sat at my house
This eternal farmer spoke to me for a while
And we discussed –
There was a good monsoon this year
                      In this part of the world
Hence the highlands have seen good yields and in the low lying areas
The paddy was bogged down under the water
Now some have reared up their heads above the water

These farmers of the world sometimes do visit me

Translation by Deepa Mukhopadhyay

Yet Some More Time

Benoy Mazumdar

I must find some more time for myself
That is what the lowest of my elements
                Endlessly urges me to do
The festering sore, that is my heart continues to burn
And yet I must carry on with life, keeping the diseases under the wrap
As discussions with flowers is ruled out, I must seek my father's help
What if I win a garland, my sickened heart, I fear
Will make water, the eternal drink, insipid and tasteless !

Translation by Deepa Mukhopadhyay

Check And See

Tushar Roy

Farewell friends, lying in the glowing furnace heat
When my waving of the kerchief of flames is over
Search through the ashes, check and see if there was any sin.

Now I no longer suffer, for I have learnt
Body means a few inevitable traditions
The body sometimes a lamp wick a puja room
Yet you didn't believe
Again and again have I ripped open my breast to
Show love, repeatedly I have pulled off my skin
Like a vest to expose muscles, sinews, and veins
After all this I have accepted defeat, farewell my friends.

Lying in the glowing furnace heat
I wave this kerchief of flames
When the fire dies out
Search through the ashes, check and see if there was any sin.

Translation by Malabika Sarkar

Then

Tushar Roy

However much perfume be used
I know that women smell just like onions
A little like fish-scale
And like an onion, layers and layers are to be peeled off endlessly

At times there is a rumbling sound in the blood
Then the springs and balances of all the watches tighten and tauten
In the circus arena the roaring tigress pounces upon the
                              Ringmaster, then————-

When the ladies laugh heartily at
The clown squirting tears,
I feel like leaping into a terrible abyss
With seven thousand horses.

Translation by Malabika Sarkar

Who Is The Hunter?

Tushar Roy

The sound of a bullet shot, a sharp pain on the right of the chest
A twisting agony in the heart, and— a breath
Nothing after that, only the cloud filled sky
                         the intense sunshine blue
Then the eagle only circling high above
And down below my shattered body
Behind the bushes that red hat with a white feather
Who is he? The hunter, or the cowherd boy
And whoever am I —who am I
Fleeing day night? Or
                     The one who today at seven o'clock in the morning
In a direct encounter tried, a bullet, sound smoke——
                             After that——
Nothing after that, then only the circling of the eagle
I cannot understand who is the killer
He or I, I or he, who is the hunter?

Translation by Malabika Sarkar

A Poem Dedicated To The Beloved

Tushar Roy

Reclining on a red divan you hardly understood
I was willing to be a thirsty deer and wade into the water
Had you desired to eat, I would have scratched out my liver
                                        And held it to your lips,
For you I was ready to be a racehorse to be betted on everyday
For one kiss of yours, I would give five lakh dinars like a Shah-en-Shah
Or exactly five kicks on an appropriate pair of ass
You hardly understood anything
You went away a meaningless yellow submarine
Carrying liquid jaggery to Mauritius

I die of wounded hopes, you———-
You hardly understood anything—deaf dumb
                                A bed - pan are you
You are a sparkling urin basin in an otherwise shabby bathroom.

Translation by Malabika Sarkar

The Stairs Of Coffee House

Samarendra Sengupta

Its now fortyfour years I had gone up and down these steps
Once, in nineteen fifty one
Manabendra Roy almost slipped on the eighteenth step
He would have fallen hadn't I caught him
Later many a time I proved myself to be humanist like this
Not exactly radical though

Many people had climbed these steps of Coffee House
Some had gone upto the first base of fame
Enrolled their names and went down
Never to climb again
On these very steps
Once I stood nonplussed to see
How Naxal Gouree metamorphosed into congress Mukherjee
Its love that at the cost of two cups of coffee spreads its empire
For three hours over any table
Its here that Eucleid Benoy tried to explain
Why real egrat flies when man comes near
Equivocating in true Jibananda style
Its here that adroit Mallinath proclaimed
In nineteen seventyone
"Poetry will not make things happen, you know
Lets better move to Metiabruz
And buy pistols from the sailors
For this country which has gone to hell
If at least one of the class-enemies ....

By and by one day
Love comes to an end
Revolt revolution within a decade
Reduces the dense hair of youth
To the baldness of middle- age
The knowledge that money is not soil
Makes the dream-struck young man
Leave his dream behind and look into the mirror
Not his country but the cool comfort of the fridge
Is more important to him now
And love ends in the caution of condoms
In the final resolution

Forty four years.. more than three decades
Almost close to the fourth
Everything has changed
As you climb those veritable stairs
Poetry beats her breast and laments
Where are you gone, mycountry, my love?
I can feel nothing but brick and mortar
Beneath my feet

Translation by Bandana Sanyal

Quarter To Twelve

Samarendra Sengupta

Just before dying Picasso named Apollionaire

He was gasping for words then
Wind no longer cares to return to the lungs of the man
Who had painted for us
Sunshine of so many shades
Women of various hues, seen and unseen
The blue transparency of sea- rich sailor !
Glancing for once at his wife
He told his physician friend
'You never married, never studied women
You are not complete, Barnal!'
Those were the last audible words of Picasso
His daughter Kathreen stared unwinking at her father
Beside was her mother Jaqueline, whom he legally married
Onle a few years before, both cried out
'No ! You have no right to leave us like this..never'
(Art has left the painter quite sometime ago
he sat silent with his brushes, sketched listlessly on the paper
but couldn't finish a single painting)
A rose-creeper swung outside his window
Which he once planted with his own hands
Alas! Is he the same Picasso who once shook the universe?
Whom the earth's air refuses to help anymore?
To alleviate the breathing trouble
Dr. Barnal came with an injection at eleven -fortyfive and found
Picasso's heart beat had stopped

Its just quarter past eleven by my watch now
I am trying to rebuild the death scene of Picasso
Standing on the top of the Eiffel tower
The Seine flows below
There stands Louvre
From where yesterday I stole a snapshot
Of the Ship Captain
Belonging to Picasso's blue period...
Did he see Appollinaire just before his death!
Did the giant of a genius, at his last moment,
Want to approximate the poet of infinity ?
Blue with jealousy and joy
I begged Kabita Sinha, my friend, who stood beside me
'Take the last shot of my camera, please
Of Paris and Picasso and me together

The negative of Picasso
Lay in the left of my breast
Already

Translation by Bandana Sanyal

He Came And Stood

Samarendra Sengupta

Right in the middle of Park Street
Stood a teenage beggar
In soiled indecent clothes –
Beyond which
A pair of mysterious pre-adolescent eyes
Glistened in expectation
In the light of neon lamps
He was staring at the crowd
Male and female figures
Under clothes of different measures
He could hear the crooner's voice
Following the gentleman
Who has just come out of the bar
In remorseful inebriation
Her voice and the sound of the accompanying piano
Rippled like the rustic river he used to know

The word teenager is an unhappy prefix to beggar
Yet as I was dropping the smallest coin of my pocket in his box
I noticed above the dirty clothes two absent eyes
Looking at the teddy boy of his own age
Protien-fed tall and metallic bright
As he stretched his begging hands at me
Perhaps he was thinking .. what?
I don't know
Only once he turned his face to me
As the coin that I dropped
Tinkled in his box

For a moment he looked at me
The drunken wretch
Knocking at the door of ale-houses
Drowned in drinks, yet searching the river
Searching in vain
Again and again

Translation by Bandana Sanyal

The Wooden Chair

Amitava Dasgupta

Sitting too long on a wooden chair
One turns into wood
His toenails send roots down the floor
His waist oozes gum
Of Sundari and Garan tree
That stick him fast to the planks
Krr..rr, Kr..rr..rr
The wood-borer bores
Through his heads to his toes
As he turns into wood
Completely so –
Sitting too long on the wooden chair

Then,
When someone slaps him on the face
He does not react
Woman comes in complete surrender
He does not stir
The infant toddles towards him
He does not stretch his hands
Plank after plank
He is a perfect wooden chair now
In every joint of his body
Sing the rusty nails
Sings the roving wood-borer
Sings the restless saw

His hands which once ruled the ocean
Are two heavy handrests now
Of his two knees that galloped like two chestnut-brown horses
The left doesn't know now when the right is severed
Wood doesn't know tears or dreams
Can not sleep or wail
With little efforts could have seen from the window
Men toiling like camels—
Tall men, short men, men of medium height
So many of them!
The problem is he can not walk to the window side
And there is the rub

Only,
His eyes also nailed to the wood
Dreams of growing into bigger chair
For the rest of his life
From the small to the large
And then to the larger and larger

Translation by Bandana Sanyal

I am India

Amitava Dasgupta

Bullets from the stengun riddled my breast
And the map that the bullet marks outline
Its name is India

With every drop of my blood
In the teagardens, coffee plantations
In coalmines, hills and jungles
Love that was scribbled
Its name is India

The dream of bumper harvest
Of endless songs
That was sown in the rough and rugged soil
Sterner than a murderer
Irrigated by my tears
Manured by the phosphate of my bones
Its name is India

Now on my cold countenance congealed
The solemn shadow of the stony dykes
Of Bhakra-Nangal
The oil that wells
From the bosom of Digboi
Like mother's milk
Flooded my body
Militant workers
Rushed from the cottonmills of Ahmedabad
To clasp me in their bossom

Wiping the blood of riots from my forehead
My corpse is today guarded by so many sentinels
The plough bearing Balaram's
The wrath not sorrow of every raped tribal woman
Set my funeral pyre on leaping flames.

Clouds like fullgrown womb
Are shaking the sky
Rains are imminent
The melting snow of gangotri
Will flow between the assassin's stengun and me
And a little later
All the dry beds of ponds and puddles
Of lakes and cannals
Will fill to the brim
Like my mother's eyes
Verdure will cover with kisses
All the naked boulders

The rhythm of Odissi dances

The beats of santhali madals
Vibrant Bhangra
Mudra of Bharatnatyam will stir up
Night of tempestuous revelry

That night
When stars will explode
In unleashed mehfil
Do not forget me

My torn limbs, severed hands, mangled bowels
And uprooted heart
Drops of tears, blood and sweat
Miles and miles of emotion and love

Name of all this is
Motherland
Independence
India.

Translation by Bandana Sanyal

Poetry And Slogan

Amitava Dasgupta

When I set about writing a poem
Arunbabu says:
'Doesn't it read like a slogan?'

When I set about writing a slogan
Barunbabu says:
'This exactly resembles poetry!'

So without paying any heed to any
I go on writing
For the rest of my life
Slogans reading like poetry
Poetry reading like slogans

Translation by Bandana Sanyal

Dhaka May 21 :1990

Amitava Dasgupta

Trudging across the birthplace of Ram
Tramping across the mosque of Babri
I am being infinitely delayed
In reaching you
Bangladesh!

So much delay
Makes all the boulders crack with deafening noise
All the rocks wear infallible stains of blood
Peeved and hurt
All the flowerbuds drop
Red, in the sunset hours

And
Hands that stretch to shake
Change to slithering snakes
Hissing and biting each other's face

And yet
We came from a village of songs and harvest
We spoke in hues of orange and green
We eyed with care the frisky 'sarputhi' fish
We had dreams
Not follidol or arsenic
In our bags.

We wanted to build the longest bridge
For the whole world to cross

Just by chaining heart with heart.

Haven't we seen
The fiery face of man turning mad in love?
Why then
Our sunlit barns get plundered at midnight?
On our shoulders grow
The surest axe of the assassin
Our beloved women
Give birth to cudgels after cudgels ?

And
Wrongful death gallop like a horse
Blowing a false trumpet?

No!
We don't want to get scorched by any more false hopes
We don't want again to mistake the face of a brother for a murderer
For the red fire engines are ringing all around
Like intense pain

For
The split throat of a century's last decade
Spills blood in iterant splashes

For trudging and tramping through
The birthplace of Ram and Babri Mosque
We are making infinite delay
To reach you, Bangladesh !

Translation by Bandana Sanyal

Demon

Utpal Kumar Basu

The other day
I came across solitude
On Suren Banerjee road
I said, here's a letter addressed to you
I was about to post it, are you
Telepathic? When did you arrive ? By which train?

Actually it was not solitude
A new and calm comb, bought off the pavement
A long black strand of a woman's hair
Still stuck between its teeth.

Translation by Sunandini Banerjee

Breadcrumbs Off My Shirt

Utpal Kumar Basu

I told you, that day, in the basement retiring room that I had once lived on the first floor of their house. It is not, perhaps, wholly a lie, because, in those days there used to be rail tracks. Here .. a tea shop at the level crossing-, I vaguely recall, it even had some sort of a westernised name -I told the young proprietor, it was your father we knew so well- he had smiled only vaguely and pointed to a portrait on the wall decked out with a garland of dried flowers from who knows when. We used to drink plenty of tea then —and occasionally toasts. I start brushing away imaginary crumbs off my shirt, shaking off bread crumbs, pepper, large grains of sugar, black ants — one after another they fall to the ground, nineteen ninety, eighty, those last few months of sixty nine, April sixty two, winter fifty seven, Dhubulia nineteen fifty, Rashid Ali Day, the fields and farms of forty two...

Translation by Sunandini Banerjee

The Ship Sailing Away

Utpal Kumar Basu

The third day we looked out of the window
And saw, far away
A ship sailing on the waters
The dice made of stone started shaking within the threshold

The shirt hanging on a peg
Swelled up against the wind
A balloon, from the festivities of a night
Long ago
Broke away from its string
And began to bob about the room

The one whom we jokingly called a demon
In human form, spoke up—
I am not that hungry today
The peon on the cycle waved his hand at us, informing
Today there are no letters for you
Sukhomoy - babu undid the 'kerchief from
Over his bald pate, and said
It is hardly that sunny any more

On that third day, the large room in
The south was vacated. A new family moved in
They said to the landlord
We shall eat out
The boy's very reliable. He laughed and replied
Let the key remain in the lock
There was running water, all of that day

The rest of the day was spent leisurely
Beyond doubt we have identified ourselves
The women smoke in public
News of Chhotdi's husband passing exam arrived
There was heavy feasting

During that week's vacation, only one day did we
See a ship sailing far away at sea
It could be seen for
Only a few moments
Then the waves
Only, the waves

Translation by Sunandini Banerjee

My Spectral Spirit

Utpal Kumar Basu

At the border of the night
Parting of her hair glows
In the moonlight
That girl, my ghost
Has clutched hard between her teeth
This mortal world
I can hear footsteps rushing about
In the bamboo grove
A tremendous chaos, sobs—
The intricate sleep of the lotus-seated Buddha
Shatters.

Translation by Sunandini Banerjee

About Houses

Pranabendu Dasgupta

I know very little
         about houses
I have no house of my own
Or what I have
Seems like moving darkness
Inside a whale's belly
My friends are not very rich
They live in temporary holes
         Like pigeon coops.
We meet
On the co-operative fancy terraces
Those who have large houses
Give us something to eat
         They spread mercy
            from invisible fingers.

I know so little about houses
That, whenever it rains
         I feel that my motherland is dripping
With never an umbrella of my own, I get drenched
         In the throes of an
Irresistibly hungry spell
All the dogs, all the houses get wet
The starless square of silence gets wet
My heart, escaping from my body
         Basks naked in the rainy clouds.

I know so little of houses
That if I get shelter for a little while
I think I've reached home
I feel you have created this
World with some particular assurance
I feel the merry-making of friends to be
The continuous sound of terraces being set
The brickfield beside the coconut tree
Which my grandfather used to point to
Seems to be continually sending large bricks exclusively for my house
I know so little about houses.

I want you to think about this
Go to Behala and inspect some houses
Go to Granada and buy some land
                Later I'll make a garden there
You can set up a camp for destitute children
On the pretext of giving lectures, I'll recuperate
And then go back to work in dead
                earnest
Or else you yourself will blossom into
                a sprightly garden house.
I'll choose the riverside road. Laden with
Stoves, music, lunch boxes for a picnic
I'll bring the barge in.

I don't know much about a house
I don't have a home of my own
Only if I can get inside you and
                Get a home
If you welcome that newbecoming with

The leaves of a housewarming
If you open the doors
        Of your caring eyes
Then, I may yet stay back
There is no other house
        Or love for me
I know so little about houses.

Translation by Kalyani Ghose

It Is Time For Me To Go

Pranabendu Dasgupta

It has rained in the empty garden
    it's time for me to go
The morning train has run over an unmarried pregnant girl
    it's time for me to go
On an immaculate white sheet the artiste
    sat down to sing
    it's time for me to go
A broiler chicken has to be brought from the poultry
Or else there will be no meal
    it's time for me to go
The moon that rose in some Jatin Bagchi poem
    is nowhere
    it's time for me to go
There's life, over there, a little farther, billowing like a sea,
in all its joy and sorrow, love and hate,
    don't call me back
    it's time for me to go

Translation by Kalyani Ghose

The Quarrel

Pranabendu Dasgupta

There's no point in playing like
                this —
When you knit wool like one addicted
        get donations from places
Does that have any meaning either?
One can live only if there's friendship
              between equals.

Translation by Kalyani Ghose

Who – Whom?

Pranabendu Dasgupta

Who is driving out whom?
What will happen when darkness dispels?
They will meet again in the square
                of the room
Even if there is no exchange of words, at least
                there will be eye contact
Shoulders will touch, if crowded, backs will rub,
All the harsh crop of the blushing civilisation
                will hurt the hands
He who drove one out to accomplish the design
He who eliminated one from the calculations
                to win the bet
What will happen to them!
It would have been fun if one could
                only live with forgetfulness,
Hide whatever one did not like in darkness
Love - hate would have been the name of
                the game
It wouldn't have mattered had one
                got rid of the other
Who turned whom away?
When light returns though
Your own mirror will get rid of you.

Translation by Kalyani Ghose

On Some Days I feel Sad

Tarapada Roy

On some days, because I have no money on me
I feel very sad
All around me everyone seems quite affluent
On some days, because I am unwell
I feel very sad,
All around me everyone seems relaxed, healthy.

On some days I feel sad for being in love
On some days I feel sad for being out of love
On some days, because I have no friends,
On some days, because I have no enemies
On some days because I have not been complimented
Or because I have not been slandered
On some days I feel very sad.

Translation by Rolla GuhaNeogy

What Was It That I Wanted

Tarapada Roy

We met after many days
Instead of asking, "How are you?"
With folded hands I bumble, "Thank you"
These days I have become forgetful
Instead of writing an address in Delhi
I write the name of a road in Kolkata
Groping for my pocket handkerchief
I take out a matchbox instead and stand still
What was it that I wanted?
Walking absent mindedly on some days suddenly
Reach the road of my old locality
What was it that I wanted?

These days I have become very forgetful.

Translation by Rolla GuhaNeogy

The Indian Map

Tarapada Roy

I do not have much of an idea
About the Indian map
How far the sea is from Midnapore
The day after flood waters inundate Bakhargunj
Guwahati is also flooded
Why this is so
Yellow, purple, in the east and west, green
The meaning of all these colours, a million dots, with countless lines
My idea is not very clear.

I know the names, but not where the mountains are situated
Somewhere lies the mouths of rivers
Somewhere the high peaks of holy places
Somewhere the boundaries of lakes
Somewhere the black soil holds open mountains of cotton
The horizon floats in the monsoon, crops wither due to lack of rain
The picture of lions in Gir forest; the Royal Tigers of the Sunderbans.
Sometimes I see these in the news, I know exactly where they are
But still I cannot pinpoint them on the Atlas.

There is only a map hanging eternally on the walls of a dilapidated house
A naked relief map, presented by an eccentric drawing teacher
With rivers like streams of blood
Bare teeth savage dark primitive mountains
Even today I do not have a clear idea of the Indian map.

Translation by Rolla GuhaNeogy

The Cooling Machine

Tarapada Roy

Our old refrigerator is
Being taken down the stairs
From the balcony I saw
The shabby, broken-legged, battered
Our twenty-five year old cooling machine
Riding away on the pull-cart

Tatai is growing up we are shifting residence
At the same time Minati and Bijon are changing too
I'm drifting from one table to another
Propelling one pen after another
Brother- father-mother, the whole milieu of relatives,
A small piece of fish in a bowl full of soup
A slice of water melon, quarter bottle milk,
We and a refrigerator ?

The cart has pulled far away
It could no more be seen from the balcony
Many days back, under a black-berry tree
In a thatched cow shed, my grandmother
Had drawn a vermilion dot on the
Forehead of our old, but one time propitious cow
The slaughterers had taken her away

As I retreated from the balcony
I felt our refrigerator
Missed out on the vermilion dot.

Translation by Barnali Roy

The Fowler

Shaktipada Brahmachari

Suddenly he was seen in the middle of the path
He had killed the emasculated red end-chaitra sun
In a tempestuous twilight

Turn around your horse, assassin. The inheritance
Of adults
Licence to kill
Tied up in the talisman a lawful writ

Neighing ceased, the axe turned bloody
River of final twilight-
I'll be pure, having washed away the blood
If you touch the limp fingers
Like a mother.

Translation by Sudeshna Banerjee

Pour Femme

Shaktipada Brahmachari

To all the erudite scholars of the Bengali language
I pray with folded hands
For that one word
The word to define woman
Woman- not woman clothed
Nor woman corrupted by a civilization of artifice, adept at making up words
Woman- naked, bare, beautiful.
Woman- desire, thirst, purification,
Sleeplessness, genesis, coition.

Words, in unending processions walk past my eyes
Banners in their hands, slogans that rack the heavens
And in that melee, nowhere can I see woman
No distinct voice in that din
A bitch astride an ass
Blind with cripple
Eunuch with old woman
I've smelt the fingers of each one
They clear their throats before they laugh
Stretch their fingers before an embrace
Exchange pleasantries before death.

Those scholars and researchers
The moralist teacher and the wily scientist
Preacher and bard—
The largest banner they carry
Has the world's most obscene letter.

Translation by Sudeshna Banerjee

Conference Of Poets

Shaktipada Brahmachari

Poems will now be read on the stage
Hence this bodes well for you
In other words you can now get up from your seat in the audience
Go out and puff at a cigarette.

And the gentleman just behind you
Who'll presently tap you on the shoulder and leave
Pretending to have remembered something urgent
He too decided
After a couple of glances at his watch and the sky above
This was the time to make way homewards
Because poems are now being read on the stage.

Respected sir, or dear sir
You too, who consider this mass exodus
A bit impolite
I've watched you too
Your over curious eyes tell it all
It was only last Thursday in the evening market
You couldn't have guessed in your wildest dreams
That the gentleman with a nylon bag in his hand
Could have been a poet!

O young friend of mine in the audience
Lower your mouth to the girlfriend beside you
Whisper in her ears
Where exactly you'll meet her
Tomorrow evening at six

Where exactly you'll wait for her
What could have been a better time
To carry on all those urgent conversations
Of your entire lifetime
Because poems are now being read on the stage.

Friends! I envy you
Because like all of you
Such opportunities once come my way
But my leaves have all dropped off in the last spring
And I realize
Amidst the confused hints of my barren branches
I, the poet on stage
Have become your adversary.

Translation by Sudeshna Banerjee

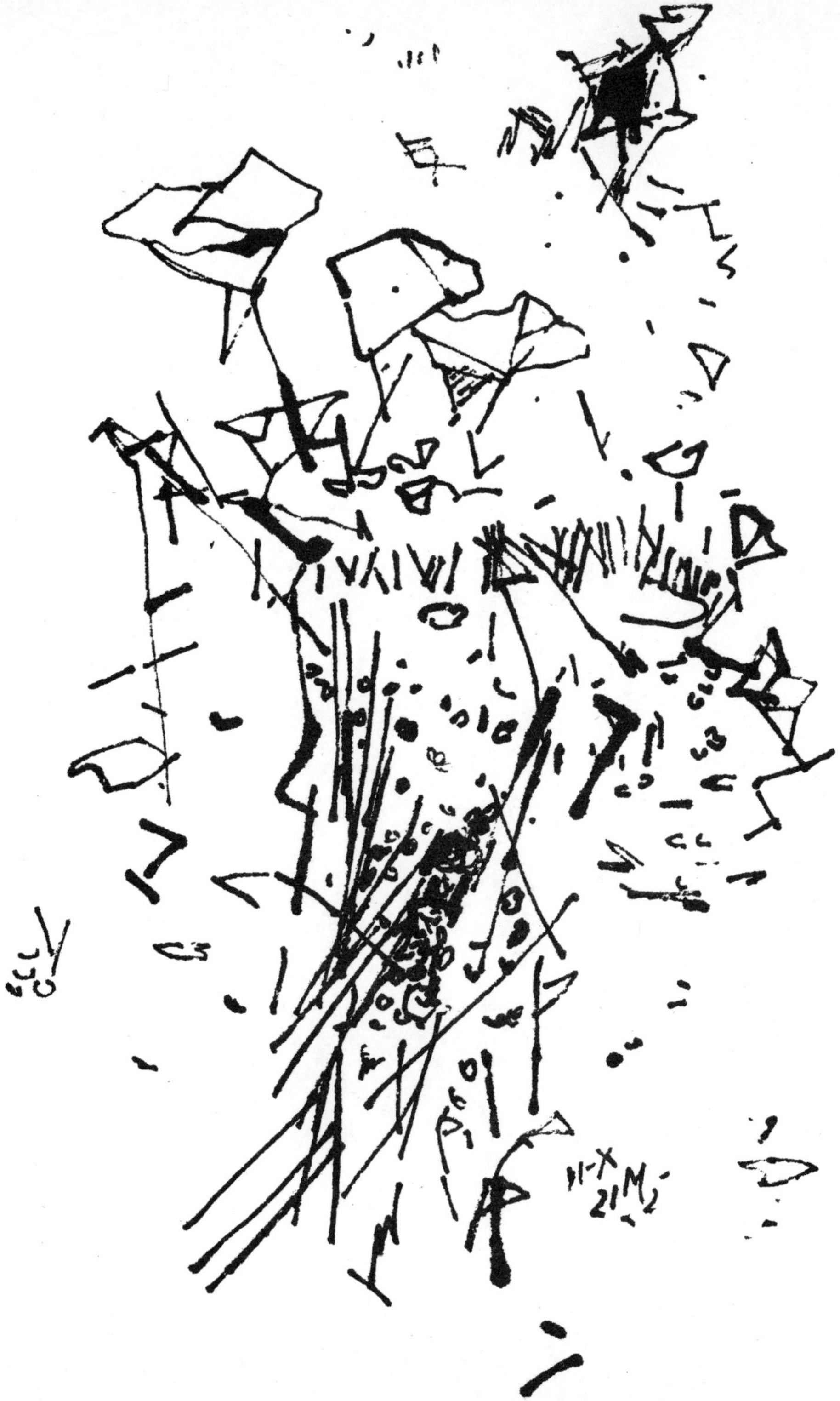

All This Play-Acting

Vijaya Mukhopadhyay

Open the curtains of the window
The sick need to see
The cheerful canvas of the skies
Etched with clouds, avenues, small square houses
Houses teeming with gossip and all this play-acting.

A lifetime of infirmity, so be it
She does not favour euthanasia
She wants her daughter to cycle about in the terrace
And not walk down the streets with that stupid boy
Bedridden, this flickering body
Desires to live and lives
By sucking in Nature's natural humidifiers; so
The leaves shed from the trees, the colour fades from the clouds
Houses teem with gossip
And all this play-acting.

Translation by Sutapa Neogi

Advertisement

Vijaya Mukhopadhyay

It is possible to have an abortion five times
So the advertisement claims.

Then why did she weep
When she miscarried at six weeks?
Why did her tender breasts
Darken at the nipples?
In the womb the bloody hand
Eclipses the growth of a cuddly child
O devil woman, you will not be spared
The female foetus will return again and again
And again and again you will return
Anxious, to that putrid clinic

Translation by Sutapa Neogi

Equation

Vijaya Mukhopadhyay

At the end of the day I sit face to face with you
Hoping the heat to be off
The oil crackles till it is ready
As it hots up the noise stops, all is quiet.
This is the time for settling scores
All I see is you, your face, even with eyes shut
High time to brush off indignity
To outstrip you, leave you behind.
But then the surging milky way changes colour
Dark steps come up blocking the earth
Bidding time for the game uphill
Forgetting all else, stupefied, I try
To perceive your equation, your zero
To realize what clips my wings
Also to find who is stronger of the two

Translation by Enakshi Chattopadhyay

Out Of Raghuvamsha

Vijaya Mukhopadhyay

Air borne is his chariot, Ram, leaving Lanka
With Sita, heads for Ayodhya.
She watches the various clouds glide by
From the open window of the air plane
Some darting down, brushing the palm tops
The green mosque minarets. Some rush
As though to swallow the Pushpak
Janaki stretches her arm for the clouds
Only to be rewarded with a bangle of lightening strokes...

At last, at long last she is happy.
Trees, clouds, ocean, earth have offered her friendship
Raghupati is beaming
What more can one want than the company of the dear ones.

This rare moment, precious and magnificent
Is from Raghuvamsha,
Far, far away from trouble-torn Ayodhya.

Translation by Enakshi Chattopadhyay

Montu's Day

Manibhusan Bhattacharya

Even in this dead city
Leaves sprout, flowers bloom, butterflies flutter
And in golden sunlight a sweet fruit or two
Appear high above.

Midday. In the dustbin the crows hold a conference
Chaired by a street cur,
With long whiskers, a couple of bound notebooks
Watch on the right wrist, cigarette in the left hand
Sons of babus emerge
From goddess Lakshmi's chest of stolen treasure
To oil the fair feet of goddess Saraswati
And just then —

The glass tumbler slips from Montu's hand.
Kalipada tightening his waistcloth gets up from the chair
And kicks him hard on the arse.

Keeping the spoon down on the plate, the college teacher
Lifts his indulgent eyes from the Amritabazar
Takes off his specs, lightly removes from the mouth end
A bit of omlette with the tip of his tongue
 Swishes it in and says,
"Oh Kali, why do you strike so hard—
Say what you like
Poultry eggs are not so tasty."

Montu groans, lying prostrate on eggshells
Rotten tea leaves, enticements of Five Year Plan
And the editorial of Anandabazar
Tears roll down his cheeks.

"You bastard Montu, stop acting, get up and slice bread."
Montu cuts bread. He cuts a quarter pound right in the middle
Toasts it, spread cream on it, serves D.M. Nathu babu,
D.M. that is Debendra Mohan—earning a fortune from
Sale of iron rods got off goods train——-
Now a civic councilor.

At five in the morning Montu lights the earthen stove
Places the ghugni bowl on it and cleans utensils with sleepy eyes
Fresh buckets from Lalgola passenger on their way to the market
The moving shadow of Hilsa with heads stuck in ice
Tails up, Montu washes cups and saucers
Staring at the apple hanging from a string at the shop-front.

Babus arrive one by one-Amritabazar and Anandabazar
Drift from table to table. Montu wipes the long knife
On a dirty cloth, slices bread with four hands
Spreads cream and serve one to Keshab babu the godown owner
Another to the labour leader Dinabandhu
Spreads butter for the headmaster Biplab babu
Cream for the reporter Tarun Mukhujjay
Cream for Nandi babu, butter-Talapatra, butter- Ghosh babu
Cream -Samajpati, cream, butter..... cream butter cream butter.

Nothing but stale rotten ghugni is left for Montu
But though he cuts bread in two and gives away to two persons
One thing is left in his hand
Like a sudden lightning leaping on the dark sky of India
An eight-inch long shining knife.

Translation by Santa Bhattacharya

The Story Of The Martyr's Day

Manibhusan Bhattacharya

Mahim of our neighbourhood sells joss sticks.

Days pass, nights come, the Ganga around the decayed slum
Dreams of Farakka
Roti-induced sleep descends, from the land of stars
With jute cot on its head
The moon was not yet up on the dark fortnight
The railway colony was still silent
Ten bundles of thin sticks and a little aromatic powder
Make offerings for gods
Father died of paralysis, mother suffers from TB
The younger sister whispers in the dark
His only secret pride- the younger brother
Sometimes comes at midnight, has meals
The workers of the jute mill enquire about the brother
With deep concern
But the sudden sound of boots beyond the gaps in the fences
Chills the blood in the mother's heart
Mahim in our neighbour hood makes joss sticks.

The' revolutionary' of yesterday is today's minister
Out of ministership he becomes a chameleon leader
Yesterday's killer is today's project planner
Villages depopulated in drought- thousands lie on the railway platform
People die of starvation. "Malnutrition deaths "
Writes Anandabazar
Stars come and go leaving shadows, sometimes it drizzles
Our neighbour hood Mahim appears with lighted joss sticks

On the train or on the over bridge.

With stubby beard and moustache
Unclean Pajama and striped shirt
Covering his remarkable physique
A bulging sling bag, stifled roar in eyes
Mahim lights a joss stick and perfumed he goes around
Among men. The odour of their bodies dispelled
Only the odour of the mind hidden all day
The babus attend office; the cine club is in full swing
And in the head Marx and dying joss sticks
Swing right to left.
What accumulates under the carefully pleated punjabi
Is not salt but hidden perspiration full of hypocrisy
There is blast in the sun and the earth experiences
Many a Vietnam- big and small.
Days pass, nights come along the vast expanse of the sunset
Thousands of boys are red with fresh blood. In many hard
Angry torches of stars break the horizons of the night
Floating in the fire of the dawn, the tired muscles made taut
Mango black–berry and neem trees are filled with sunbeam
Nurturing in his breast the secret dream of his brother
Sells lighted joss sticks our neighbourhood Mahim

Translation by Santa Bhattacharya

Night At Gandhinagar

Manibhusan Bhattacharya

Everybody knows Gokul. The D.I.B. man notes him
Looking askance in between reading the Statesman
As darkness thickens, Gokul's mother says,
" No more, go away now."
Before he could return, the flash of khaki at the door
The revolver thunders, Gokul roars
The greyhound of the state bends and tears off a patch of hair
To the eyes of the night -blind mother
Battle of Kurukshetra, brass of the belt, boots
Darkness descends in torrents
The circle of death, time eternal, the spacious field
Grief of the colony's Subhadra rumbles in stones.

The college teacher said," That's wrong, why take the law in your hand?"
The schoolmaster coughs, "Where's revolution?
Only a multitude of the abject poor died."
The lawyer was wary," I didn't take biscuits
Enter only the price of tea."
Chhokumian of the jute mill, "This time I'll thrash the scoundrel O.C."

The earthen stove remains unlighted. Close to the fences
Runs the bubbling blood stream of that dare devil
Stars in the twilight sky were overshadowed by cloud.

Translation by Santa Bhattacharya

He Who Is Alone

Pabitra Mukhopadhyay

He who is alone is not alone, even
His feet are planted on the ground
You can rip up roots
Unknowable pain racks the body

He who is alone is not alone, his
Wishes are asleep in body cells
The burden of a momentary despair
Hisses in terrible rage

Does anyone stay? No one stays
The chill collects over frozen snow
To repay its debt to the fire
That too in its own time

Whatever he takes spreading his hands
Words, mundane gifts
He gives away as he goes
Vain glory of the subconscious

Whatever he does from hurt pride
Grief or distress towards humanity
He brings home far more,

To think one is alone is self-love

Translation by Sriparna Basu

To A Dead Friend

Pabitra Mukhopadhyay

You thought, you were alone; above you no
 Shelter, no tree
The tree under which you could wait for the storm to pass
You found its trunk affected by decay
The friend whose shoulder you leaned on
Thinking this is how you could walk a long way
Without fear, at some point
He also stopped lending you his shoulder
You could not walk alone
I'm walking even though alone
The tree I'm waiting under
Is desolated by falling leaves
Its trunk too affected by decay
The friend whose shoulder I leaned on, he too
 Sat down travelling some distance. By now
In so many days
Perhaps his body too is covered under dust

And I'm walking, The Pied Piper Of Hamelin
How many shades behind me; They are flesh and blood, they are
alive

Translation by Sriparna Basu

Politics

Pabitra Mukhopadhyay

The girl was adamant- it is him that
I'll marry; her groom dumb, let
That be, - he could not
Order her around
Said the father - Think it over, who
You can talk to, who
will pick roses, open
windows to moonlight, teach
the bird to speak, greet
the guest
who will explain to you the portends
of dreams!

The girl had lost her mother, early, so
Father had poured his love, distraught
Lest she regretted the loss, indulging
Her little whims and fancies

The girl said, - let it be, his
Desires would mean, chains on
My desires; let
My wishes be his wishes

The groom is happy- a princess spread over his bed; lest
She minds, he obeys
All her directions, he
is impatient to
do her bidding

The girl is happy, - the groom
does not speak, he listens, and
sees,- her own
wishes stand their ground, when
can he slip golden slippers
on the goddess's feet-
he waits

Translation by Sriparna Basu

Of Defeated Humanity

Pabitra Mukhopadhyay

From the body of defeated humanity rises
Death's smell, wafts in the wind
Silently enters the existence of
Others

The smell is too familiar to us like
The mangy dog or the pet cat of
a domestic household
(Do I always emit that smell into
 the wind when I walk?)

I was supposed to fly high touching
The cathedral's spine
Bring divine food to assuage the grief
Of hungry days of the ever-destitute
Hand it over- to those hands in whose
Cracks lurk the merciless empty lands
Of summer drought, bloodless,
Hand over to them a hundred and
eight blue lotuses, the untirng
Festival of harvest
I too will be victorious, snatch with
This hand wealth and boundless
Longevity
Whatever has been made by man and
Nature - I will take compassion,
Love, ferocity, mercy
The man who floats and crashes with

The crest of a wave knows no defeat
He lives, drowns his home but
Sets it up again, tears bonds
Casually lives and dies
His body does not smell of death
Spreads in the wind the white pollen of
Flowers
We know that smell too, we too
Waft it in the wind when we walk

Translation by Sriparna Basu

My Being : Embryo

Geeta Chattopadhyay

On the other side of the river, a village
A crematory on this bank
Newborn, will you go, or stay?
Smeared with funeral ashes like apathy
                        The newborn turns hermit
Shapeless head crippled hands, with crimson bloody
Palms enfolding the fruit of sorrow make an exit—
The bamboo cracks noisily on the skull of night
The funeral flames lick up the body, pitch dark night
Dancing with sari abondoned, by the riverside
This the crematory, the village, across the river—
Newborn, will you go or stay back? Oh, but he goes!

Translation by Malabika Sarkar

Birth

Geeta Chattopadhyay

"Will you play with dolls anymore?"
On the forehead he smeared a red mark
"Will you venture across the threshold again?"
The hands he bound with bangles of shell
" Will you be late at the ghat?'
The two feet were strongly outlined with alta.

And the pangs started then
Inside the dark caverns of art.

Translation by Malabika Sarkar

Ocean To Himalayas

Geeta Chattopadhyay

From the ocean to the Himalayas
Lay stretched that stale corpse
Pelted with the nightmarish onslaught of terrorist steel
The heart in a few pieces, the left lung shattered
No spleen or river, the invisible upper jaw
The kidney alone left and the stomach all over space
Before the explosion he hadn't eaten for four hours—
Only the feet unhurt wore a pair of sports sneakers
Surrounding the overturned body a river of blood
Breathless, the lower jaw parts slightly to say "Aaa"—-
When interviewed by a freelance photographer.

With a sandalwood garland in hand belt jacket bomb
Approaching, some with heavy plastic and smuggled
            RDx 9 volt batteries
Strapped on their shoulders
Targeting only me, Ocean to Himalayas.

Translation by Malabika Sarkar

Burning Of The Sati

Geeta Chattopadhyay

The dog crossed the knee-deep brimming water
The line streaming from the eyes, that is your river Baitarini
Infested with poisonous ants, the body shrouded with water apple branches
Steel grips forcing you down in case you've a change of mind
Here you'll be cremated, and now to ascend to the pyre
Here you'll be cremated, and now to ascend to memories
Here you'll be cremated,- blood red lips, lotus navel
Lift the cloth from the face and see for the last time
                              Your husband!

Translation by Malabika Sarkar

You Too, God

Piyush Raut

A lawyer will travel to Agartala by the
Tripura Road Transport bus today. He is obligated to
A covenant of a few thousand rupees.

Probable outcome is poor Rakhahari Das
will be hanged or exiled soon.
His offence -he has killed a plump goat of his neighbour Anwar Hossain
More serious accusation-he instigated Hossain's wife for a divorce.

Conforming to the Jury, The Judge ordered the convict Rakhahari Das
To be imprisoned for life according to Art. 301 of the Constitution.

A few gallons of foreign liquor was gobbled down
By midnight. A nightlong jubilation and revelry at the club.

In a faraway lonely captive camp
A weak Rakhahari in his bloodshot eyes and fluffy face
Murmured to himself- but God, I have not done any wrong!
God, epitome of aloofness, as if he had not heard nor seen anything
Walked dispassionately into the huge club of Anwar Hossain
And with an elegant wine glass in hand
Drank to everybody's health.

Translation by Barnali Roy

The Prelude To Revolution

Piyush Raut

I have a burning fancy to
Tear open all dresses, crush
The face of Goddess Durga.
When I go to pick fresh vegetables
I find my small piece of land covered by rat holes all over.
The river evaporates like a mirage
As I try to fetch water.
And thus the seed of revolution starts sprouting in my mind.
I feel like throwing a slick poisonous snake
Into every couple's bed.
There's nothing called sin or piety
And yet, surprisingly, an unfair balance sheet is repeatedly
Held before our eyes, by none other than
Our Father.

Translation by Barnali Roy

About Him

Piyush Raut

He stood all through the summer
With a smile on his lips
His dress is blue. His two huge hands held
Love for us all

He was told-A sea-faring ship will
take you abroad. Will you like to push on ?
He never answered. Only smiled

Summers have receded. The fog all over
Bursts into rainfall
The psyche warns us of
Unnatural death from iceberg.
Our frail and coarse bodies are replete with
Poisonous splinters.
Then from the oblivion he announces-
Beseech Me.
His blue dress used to sparkle in fire
But never got burnt
His huge hands held love for us all
He was told of the sea-faring ship
Willing to take him
Will you travel?
He never answered. Only smiled.

Translation by Barnali Roy

When Will Winter Come, Suparna

Bhaskar Chakrabarty

When will winter come Suparna I'll sleep for three months
Every evening someone jokingly injects frog's blood
Into my veins - I sit still - in the dark
They float blue balloons, burst crackers all through the night
Hullabaloo - then suddenly
Like magic all the candles go out - the festive day
Like breeze, rushes to the other side, the sound of flute
Cannot be heard - then the very sight of water makes me want to jump
To immerse my body in water
And hold my head out high all through and breathe
I don't like it Suparna, I
Am not human, not light, not a dream - my feet
Is gradually becoming wide - horses' hoof beats
Give me palpitations, my breath becomes short I push
The hands on the clock forward with my finger every day
I don't like it - winter
When will it come Suparna I'll sleep for three months

Once, as soon as I woke up at dawn I saw a lowering cloud
Near the window - it was dark all around
Couldn't even see my own nails then - the day
I cried as I remembered you - burnt my hair
With a match and went to sleep amidst the smell of burnt hair
Now I'm not like a human being - as I walk along the road

I suddenly feel like jumping - up to love, those long three months
I don't feel like sitting with my head bowed down
As soon as I hear human footsteps, I feel breathless,
I run back the way I came - why run back? I don't like it
when will winter come Suparna I'll sleep for three months

Translation by Bidisha Basu

For The Lost Youth

Bhaskar Chakrabarty

Oh missing youth
By now you must have seen the ads
In the daily papers.

I do not know where you are
In the mountains, or the seas
In a seventeen-storied hotel or in a slum.

Are you roaming the streets
Of this pin - filled Calcutta?
Clutching a few day old notes left by you
(Bring the shirt and pants back from the laundry)
Your sister sits sullen
Nowadays, does anybody really
feel pain for another?
In this world of suppressed tears
I want to make friends with you
You done well to move away
From the talons and masks.
The tears from your eyes may now be
Inviting pearls, - are you dead
Or alive? If at all you're still
Alive - my friend, never come back home.

Translation by Bidisha Basu.

Another Love Poem

Bhaskar Chakrabarty

We meet again after so long - on a winter evening
Come let us go shall we ?
Is marriage still such an event?
I still wish to walk quietly by your side
Trees lining the streets- in isolation - do they still want us?
I have spent days and I have spent nights- dreamless...
Only with dreams,
Has the winter wind ever played havoc with you?
Have you spent sleepless nights alone by the window?
Look, look, it has started to rain; why haven't you wrapped yourself up
properly?
Now I'm no longer mad ———-
Now I have tablets and trams, Calcutta, blank faces of men, happy and sad
We shall meet again after along time
When you are busy talking about your husband
I pocket a snapshot of you, alone, standing next to a "nooliya",
I guess I shall never return it to you.

Translation by Bidisha Basu

Death

Bhaskar Chakrabarty

When death stands at your doorstep
What do you do?
What do you do?

Do you tremble?
Hand over the bank papers to your wife?
Ask for water?

I have almost lived my life
As I had looked at it
As I had imagined it.

Yet mistakes and confusion
Remain a - plenty.
So much remains totally unsaid
So many jokes unshared.

A real row is looming large in life
But what can one do?
Should I call my daughter to me?
A few more days of living
would be nice.

Translation by Bidisha Basu

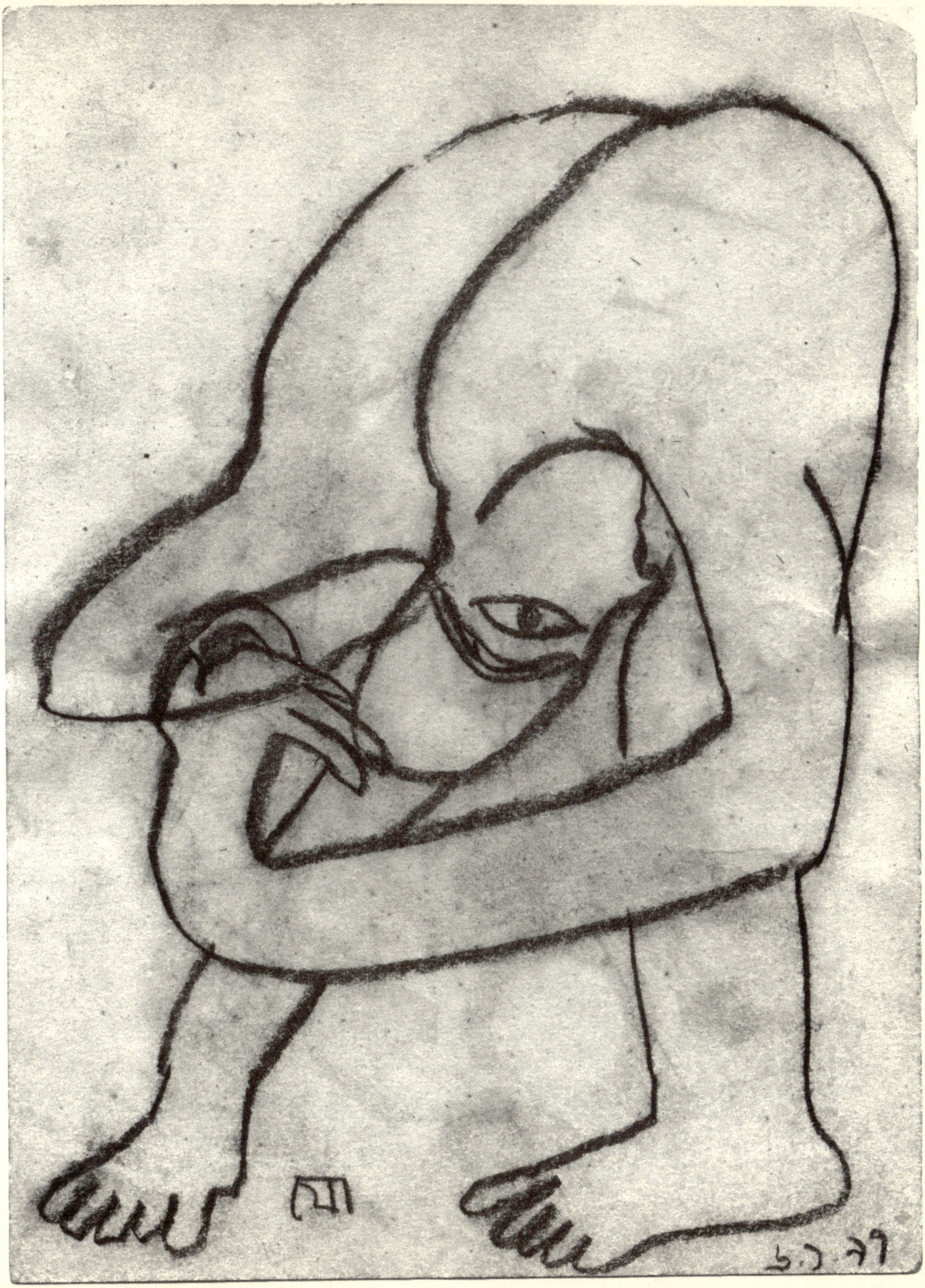

Motion

Debarati Mitra

As I placed my foot upon the stair
The house fluttered its wings
And took to flight, like a teal
Leaving not a feather behind.

I fell asleep roaming through the streets
Under the trees I woke up to see
The bokul tree with its shade
Afloat on the clouds
Like an airhostess' tiny handkerchief.

Suddenly, the wind moaned around me, raising
A breastfull of dust like the heartache of a grass covered field
Leaves and specks of straw,
Like drops of water flung around by a little spring
"Where are you going with the thunderstorm insetting?"
There was no response, no reply
My sister faded into the sky
Like the blaze of a meteor's broom-tail

Only my feet are rooted to the ground.
Does the little ant that crawls
On the deck of ship,
Ever really go on a cruise?

Translation by Sunandini Banerjee

Applied Mathematics

Debarati Mitra

That two and two make four
I do not believe anymore
Two added to another two
Can result in a piglet
Or even the atom bomb's Manhattan project.
Over there the sun
Like a fish
Flying free of the fishing line
Is disappearing into the bottom of the river,
And that boy is picking cabbages
Like a shadow that lies
Cheek to cheek with the horizon
A train chug-chugging
Moves slowly into his ken
The sum total
Is evening?
But there is no common denominator
To any of the above.

Two couples are talking for 45 minutes-
They cannot be husband-wife, or
Ordinary lovers
Not brother-sister, nor keya blossoms-srabon month.

Then who are they?
I do not want to keep account
Of the breeze
Nor of the clock.

If to the colour blue
The route of the flying bird is added
Will it result in the sky?
If to the reflection in the mirror
A sigh is added

Translation by Sunandini Banerjee

No, No And No

Debarati Mitra

There's no hurry
If you say this isn't the time
I'll agree to wait
No longer the mirror
In you a translucent curtain
The candle's fairy with her small bright tongue
Licks the sweet darkness.
Alone, I watch from afar
A strain of the cricket's song wafting towards the balcony.

A nobody, I know I'm not anybody
Yet I remain waiting
If I can hear your hand suddenly opening a window-
That face like white fulsome clouds
If they become waves plunging into my sea
The eye rests once
On the pared nails, a few remote stars
Whose rays haven't yet reached this sky.

There's no fear, but is there no hope too?
There are countless lives yet-
As insects, animals, vegetation, sand and stone
I don't object to any-
I'll stay close to your footsteps
I want to hear how many times you say no
How many times you can say no.

Translation by Sanjukta Dasgupta

Omega Point

Amitava Gupta

Love survives
Lurking between land and water
Like a girl with a shadowy existence.

Hardly extraordinary, but I still noticed
A light, like that of a hazy dawn
Which arose announcing a promise.

Omega point? There are the clouds like
 her conchshell bangles
And there, each cloud throbbing
With her unspoken heartache.

She who can be loved, she
Who can be beckoned with beauty
And emptiness
Let her take my shame.

Translation by Sunandini Banerjee

Bengali

Amitava Gupta

This language spread out through the skies
This language, both light and dark womb

At dawn when no one else
is awake, of marriage
Hover over the child's warbling.

I am the fire in her womb,
I am the streak of vermilion on her lustre

Translation by Sunandini Banerjee

Arjun: To Karna

Amitava Gupta

I am holding on to your shadow, are you
Not adept at abducting souls
Like I am? I have trapped you in the crevices
Of a restless raaga, because you were vanquished, by then,
In between smithereens of darkness
On a battlefield already half lost
I shall drive your chariot wheels
Down into the mud.
And the sun shall drown amidst a sea
Of clouds, suddenly
I know, that too is Krishna's cunning
The moment I stretch my hand towards
Your shadow,
I realize it is not I
But you who have stolen me away.

Translation Sunandini Banerjee

Yudhistir: To Kunti

Amitava Gupta

Suddenly
I wake up at the sounds of the storm
The strange glow of this dusk of disaster
Torment my eyes
When you look at me
Do you actually remember him?

The priest, the ritual altar, even the fire
Is ready
I am naked before the river thirsting for rain
Pristine am I
The offering is ready but still
Speak to me of Karna

The shade of whose spirit am I?
Whom do you kill?

Translation by Sunandini Banerjee

Hymn To The Goddess

Krishna Basu

From the beauty parlour emerged the attractive fertile idol, having erased the rural sindoor from her hair parting. Some crack jokes, some acclaim you, all hover around you like clever songs applauding your elusive beauty, dirty propositions are poured into the roots of your intense ear. Recalling the ancient image some cry uncontrollably- observing all this from far and near, from within and without, I feel like bursting out in laughter. Your ancient image in sankha and sindoor is not your true image; today's sensational, modern, sleeveless presence is not your real nature; sometimes a slave since birth or sometimes a desirable doll- who has made you? No great artist named God, such a great artist can never perform such mean jobs. Man has made you, man, man...whose height is never more than a little over six feet at the most. Once, now, for the final time construct your clay image, ignite the lamp of creativity from within yourself, look at your ten-armed beauty, Asur-annihilator. Look, at your clay feet lies the benumbed, masculine earth, drunken with the alcoholic haze of dominance. Who spat on you, who praised you, do you, care for these any more? Grow out of the small, dull space dictated by others, hold ten weapons in ten arms, stand firmly with your two feet on lion power, let us look at you, Woman.

Translation by Sanjukta Dasgupta

A Woman's Corpse

Krishna Basu

Just at the culvert-end a trapped corpse
A woman's corpse
It lies trapped, unable to let go
Her face is turned towards her child
Her face is turned towards her family
Her face is turned towards her man
That man who had battered her incessantly
Her face is turned towards him.

Foolish, petulant, care-hungry face
Even today it is turned towards life.

Just at the culvert-end a trapped corpse
A woman's corpse
It lies trapped, unable to let go.

Translation by Sanjukta Dasgupta

Your Girlchild

Krishna Basu

Imagine that your only daughter has grown up
Now she is a slim girl
She stays in the girls hostel at Santiniketan
She sings, paints and in-between classroom lessons
She gazes at the *Khoai* afar, is scolded sometimes
She weeps alone in the late night
So that her senior room mate doesn't hear her
Her silent salt tears just moisten her pillow.

It's four years today, since you two were divorced
Your self-conceit grew bigger than your own selves
So big that this small girl child couldn't reach it.
You two are busy with pleasurable girl friends
Or charismatic boy friends, ladders of success with these
You are besotted nowadays
Who was responsible; who had violated vows " Your soul is mine own…"
She is unaware of it all.
Still a young girl she hasn't yet learnt the facts of life
Had you learnt them too?

Only at night at the girls' hostel when the lights go off
The young girl's weeping, hushed groans
Her desire to give herself up turns to water and
Quietly streams on the pillow.

Translation by Sanjukta Dasgupta

Just An Ordinary Mail

Krishna Basu

At your lotus-feet, dear mother
I don't know how you are
I'm not well, not well at all.
Shall I quit all and go away, dear Mother?
Who will I turn to, tell me who will take me?
You too have taken refuge in my elder brother's family
' I'll bash your face in' your son-in-law
Roared last night, slapped me hard
No Mother, it's true he hasn't yet struck me with a shoe
But he said he will some day.
Why did you marry me off, O mother dear?
Just for being a handmaid why did you send me away
Wrapped in bridal benarasi and anointed with scented sandalwood
I've lived in this household for fifteen years
Serving and serving and keeping quiet
I just wanted to know the truth from him
Where does all the money from the salary disappear?
Just wanted to know as a matter of common right
Instantly' Shall bash your face in' he threatened
Dear Mother who will I turn to
Chhoton and Toton are yet very small
How can they give me any support, tell me?
My home before marriage, my home after marriage, tell me
To which house do I have any right of my own?

Mother dear, who will I turn to?
Or shall I just keep quiet, cook and be beaten
Serving a life sentence as 'Jewel of a woman'?
Dear mother, tell me, do I have a home of my own?
Do women have their very own homes, ever?

Translation by Sanjukta Dasgupta

April

Ranajit Das

April had appeared on the calender .. the month of my birth
I had set it down in my diary this year;
And said .. I am terribly lonely, do keep me company for the next thirty days

In the fifties you had seen my mother carrying her would be child
Tell me that story
In the fifties you had seen Jibanananda writing poetry
Read that poem to me
And come to see .... through what disastrous times my life is passing

You are not responsible for my birth, only its witness
You have seen me in happier times .. my long childhood
I have forgotten all the limericks I learnt then
Recite those rhymes to me
And come and see ... how I am continuously receding into
Toothpastes, books and Bengali cinema

Foolish April, impassive April, that does not speak, instead
Sit tight on the pages of the diary ..illiterate;
Only, after departing like my shy youngest uncle
It hands over through the month of May a new toothpaste, and
Sends a new Penguin publication about troubled times.

Translation by Rolla GuhaNeogy

International

Ranajit Das

England sent me a volume of hardbound
Unwritten constitution.

France sent me a bottle of champagne with a note :
'Drink it, and embrace the nearest abstraction.'

Japan sent me a little robot which can mourn
Human woes for two minutes.

Germany sent me a wrist-watch that indicates
Only competetive time.

America sent me an exclusive revolver that is made
'To assassinate the President only', but which finally
Provokes its owner to commit suicide.

I packed all those presents in a
Coloured suitcase painted with creepers and foliage,
And set off for the remote village
Where my uncle lives –

My sole intention was to walk, all alone,
And endless distance through the muddy village-road.

Translation by Rolla GuhaNeogy

To My Father

Ranajit Das

You spent your whole life
Fighting to keep the wolf from the door.

No art, no indulgence, no detachment
Could touch you.

It is beyond me
to write about you.

You are an inch away from
The ambit of my writing –

As the power station stands
A little distance away from the city

Translation by Rolla GuhaNeogy

Smile For The Camera

Ranajit Das

We leave as evidence ——
Our smile for the camera ——
In this star – studded black album.

Eager and yet shy, symbolic yet cordial,
This smile is our ultimate mark of identity –
Our indomitable tale of beauty.
All other smiles of ours are motive-corrupt,
                we know.
That's why, dear cameraman,
At the hour of being exiled
                as undesirable aliens,
This smile only remains as our untold evidence, that
Standing in the midst of a constant deluge,
Breaking through all the barriers of fears and darkness,
Even carrying the stone-block for the pyramid
On our backs,
We still tried to express ourselves
                with a little smile.

In your album, we leave as evidence
Of that endeavour,
Our – smile – for – the – camera.

Translation by Rolla GuhaNeogy

Hunting Ground

Tushar Chaudhury

This road leads from the tropical rain forest to Savanna
You run afar, very very far
How do I draw you within my grasp?
No, you are not a deer, nor am I really a leopard
I don't want to wring your neck ; in my heart I long only for you
What is a mirage, the will-O'-the wisp of the senses?
What is a sharp razor, a far away musk deer?

'I have seen your century torn into pieces over again
Haven't I seen your century flutter like a restless Emu
within the prison of eyes, nose, ears, tongue and skin?'
Saying these words I felt as if
The feast of zebra -flesh laid out
Thanks the paw of the lioness
All around in the parkland of Savanna
Covered with elephant –friendly grass, umbrella tree, baobab and cactus
When night descends on earth, in the woody darkness
Pairs of eyes of timeless ever hungry hyenas
Burn in greed of the leftovers
It seems
All the roads from the tropical rainforest lead to Savanna

Translation by Santa Bhattacharya

Seducing Beautiful Nina

Tushar Chaudhury

My body burns, my arms melt like wax constantly
Embrace, embrace – I am really scared of the word
Whom shall I enfold in my arms? A charming clever doe
Let alone hunting, my melting arms have never seen a bow
Shall I then take myself to the murmuring woods of falling leaves?
Beneath the bed I lie on sleeps a Cobra dead silent like God
Then I'll shift myself to the time
Cotton-soft like a dishevelled bed
Seen in darkness on the horizon of magnetic circle
I'll recline on memories' pillow and delight
In the smell of the chhatim-pollens
Wafted by the naughty breeze of the late autmn

Seduce beautiful Nina ! on the height of thirst
She gave me a glass of coke and a sharp ice pick- axe
And said, "Look at this golden thigh, scale it
A wonderful icy burial awaits you"
I wish to forget Nina's riddle, watch the hexagonal
Hotel's coquetish swimming pool
I see brown women, heavy or slim white patches on their bodies
Clusters of stars on evening kamini bushes
Diamond dusts of the last night's shower on flowers
Like marks of caress still so resplendent
Their dreamy eyes still wonder-struck with sensuous pleasure

Don't you know that time is an immobile grasshopper
On the horn of a bison, come to a sudden halt
The poacher secretly waits in the grassland
And who doesn't know that I am the deer?

Translation by Santa Bhattacharya

O Life Eternal

Tushar Chaudhury

Loneliness is stark obstinate. 'Go' I say, but it just won't
Mirth is impudent. How do I drive it away ? It won't relent
Jokes in handfuls, frolic and banter, sprays of fun
Lust, naughty nights, shedding of tears, of meteors, dawn

God of destruction, take the deer flesh, throw away
Shankha and Chakra in the rubbish vat
In the dressingroom lies alone Indra's bow, pale and repentant
Handsome youth attain the paradise of hell, poisonous and sticky
Monu knows well that funeral rites being over
Man wanders in the morgue itself

Like swarming flies, pall-bearers, hankies over their noses
Look for dead bodies of relatives in the crowd
The undertaker has sinister designs
Wait, the smell of atar, confusion
As the cover is removed : mine,
What a sweet and cold face of a young girl !
A few more marks awarded to her would not have been a sacrilege
What do you say, undertaker, magistrate, relatives, suppressing sobs
Friends at crematorium, flower garlands in hand
Burn incense, pour perfume all over, say Hari
And now cremation, imprisoned in the glasscase of the hearse
Start your journey
O eternal life, your deadbody still lies unidentified

Translation by Santa Bhattacharya

The Night Wears On

Tushar Chaudhury

Nestled in feline warmth, the master and the servant roll in fun
                                                at day time
Even a gutter washed apple has a place deep in an admirer's gaze
From the boughs of narcissistic fancy bats dangle in rows thick
Pebbles and rock bits bounce off moonbeam, or say, poesy's trick

Faulted light transforms into fastest– moving darkness, the plains turn hills and slopes

Denuded trees, but three floral patterns adorn each branch
The wandering king romps back home shaking a child's rattle
As the night wears on, he ties jungle-bells on both feet
His hedious-looking queen has an otter for a pet
Her boobs are like a pair of grenades, not pomegranate
The roadside gallants wheeze out wolf whistles in the velvity night
Not far is the railway car shed
In the hospital free bed lies like a corpse the docile night; pick axes, pistol stay awake
Awake the razor, the master and the servant.

Translation by Asesh Chattopadhyay

To Friends

Parthapratim Kanjilal

My eyes were never too full of tears
My eyes got carried away by tears
My eyes were flushed away by tears
In tears my eyes evaporated and formed
                Clouds in the sky

Knowing tears can see everything

I have fire, the fire of the blind
That holds the tongue, the collar bone, the
Arms and the upper chest
Let it first be doused.

Translation by Kalyani Ghose

More Poems Of The Night

Parthapratim Kanjilal

Lorries and cars speed towards the stars, skirting the bamboo grove
The driver looks out to see where the Milky Way is.

His smile is composed, like that of men
When they give up a job after a long stint
He remembers, he needs water to cool the engine
There must be a pond nearby.

Lorries and cars speed towards the stars, skirting the bamboo grove
The stars are reflected in the pond
They will go nowhere.

Translation by Kalyani Ghose

Table

Parthapratim Kanjilal

The table,
Dusk descends in the distance.
Fruit, a dead body, office file, a broken pair of earrings
Negative prints, album, a writing pad

What should I place on you?
The chair,
It needs to be kept a little apart.

Translation by Kalyani Ghose

The Four Friends

Shyamalkanti Das

I have been colour- blind from childhood,
But what of that?
I have four friends
Who are so colourful and fine that
I have no difficulty in recognizing colours.

Let's first take my white Brahmin friend..
Incredibly large- hearted and open -minded a person,
He Suddenly one day added depth to the ashen areas of my life
With the colour and grace of a white heron -shaped flower.

Why shouldn't I mention my shy but terribly hawkish
Red Kshatriya friend?
Not only has he brought to me the strident colours of bravado—
He has also opened my eyes to the drying
Stream of royal blood.
My deep yellow Vaishya friend is totally different,
Apprehensive yet so fond of jests
Now his life is flying through the rapids
The next moment from the ravine his
Shadowy body shakes its sides and rises up—-
Only but prod him and see how
From the fifty-five fingers of his five hands
Scatter forth colours of melancholy..

Oho, I haven't till now told you about
My indomitable black Sudra friend.

Now sits this volatile man, besmirched with ash
                At the burning ghat,
The next moment he picks up dead body
                after dead body from the river.

Try to say something and towards
You will rush a scorching wind,
From the black conspiratorial neem tree will ravenously fly
A few million crows
Rotting, decomposed human heads will spread
On your face
A black melancholy glow!
You will see the bridge to the life hereafter
Moving away little by little from under your feet
As you sink into the dark deep colour of darkness.

Peacocks, the world, flowering trees are
Moving vigorously before our eyes
But no one is looking this side, at this disaster.

Translation by Kalyani Ghose

Allegory

Shyamalkanti Das

At one time you would become restless
At the very mention of a jungle. And a thrill
would make my veins all taut. Be it evening or morning,
At one time, both of us would go to the jungle.
You would not care for the pugmarks of the tigers
But for symbols amidst trees and creepers
And I? No, not fairies and elves
My temptation was somewhat for images. But before I could go for it
Mistaking the ranger on the beat clearing his throat
For an elephant's bellow
I would go into fainting fits.
You surely do not remember these now
Nor you are supposed to
Your power of vision was very sharp, when the jungle became still
You would tear the soft and fleecy night
Into pieces. And I?
I knew neither magic nor occult
I would just grow restless in my greed for more
Images within the images.

Today we both stand on
A deserted road. I can see
The night, with the bones and limbs of the jungle in tight embrace
Slowly vanishing, like a ghost, into nothingness. And you?
Your visionary eyes are really without compare.
You can see it is not night, but symbol after symbol
Running helter-skelter around us like ten winds
In ten directions. Seeing all this, I

stand in the darkness immobile. And you?
From the symbol of jungles you vanish gradually like a beautiful
Picture into a jungle of symbols.

Translation by Kalyani Ghose

O My Motherland

Shyamalkanti Das

Just beyond the barbed wire fence
Is a long unbroken wall.

Cross the wall and there is smoke
Millions of bricks are being slowly fired.

Walls walls walls again.

Laburnums, red and yellow flower
Blossom in Bankura and Medinipur.
Red dust blows in Jessore and Khulna
In the groves of Haridaspur rings the flute.

Yet, O my motherland, for fifty years
We haven't looked at each other's faces.

Translation by Kalyani Ghose

With Wood

Shyamalkanti Das

Suddenly that noon, we met
In the afternoon we ate a little
By evening we became great friends
Then, not a word more, we went to bed

We went to bed at night with the wood
I don't exactly remember the games played by the hour
I only remember the two bodies filling up with wood-mite

Come morning, it was whispered that the clouds were no more
The sky was clear, wood rubbed against wood
To create an unusual music on the
Shoal of the river...

Translation by Kalyani Ghose

Funeral Verses

Joy Goswami

The day we retrieved mother's corpse, all ablaze, from the river
Of fire, Sister, do you remember
The questions in our neighbor's eyes?

        The experts marched in, snouts outstretched,
        Hairs bristling on the back of their necks
        The headman said: Listen, here's the verdict—
        They don't have any right to cremate.

We ran away from the village that night
Mother's body on our shoulders, moon shining above
Pestilent swamps along the way
Salt and lime pits along the way

        Your breasts desiccated, my fingers
        corroded from the caustic lime
        Nothing to eat, no scope for ablution
        Our task was akin to pallbearers'

We reached a realm with dead trees everywhere
Dead animals' skins dangling from the branches
When we came to the riverbank at the end
Of the earth we put mother's skeleton down

        Sister, I swear, we won't burn these bones
        Though it's not our custom we'll hide them
        In the hollow of a tree. Won't those who
        Follow us know how to honor them?

Our bodies have grown moldy, we have
No eyes now, only sockets smarting with tears
I've forgotten whether I was ever a man
You don't remember your last show of blood

        The light in the east is skull-white
        Behind it darkens as dusk falls
        Sitting in the last burning ground on earth
        We're just a pair of body snatchers.

Translation by Carolyn Brown

Maltibala School For Girls

Joy Goswami

Benimadhob, Benimadhob, I miss you.
Benimadhob, do you ever think about me?
Benimadhob, you were beneath the tamal tree
playing your magic flute, I was doing arithmetic
sitting at my desk at Malti School, the teacher
was outside the little classroom meeting her husband

I was in Class Nine, old enough to wear a sari then
It was at Sulekha's house, Benimadhob, where we first met

Benimadhob, Benimadhob, a model student
you came from the city for a visit, I'm dark
I saw you and ran home as fast as I could
Benimadhob, my father works in a shop

And yet bees hum in the garden, buds do blossom
At studies in the evening my arithmetic goes wrong
I was in Class Nine, Iwas sixteen then
Our first rendezvous, Benimadhob, was beside the bridge

Benimadhob, Benimadhob, after so many years
Tell me honestly, do you still remember ?
Have you told your girlfriend all this?
I saw her with you just one time
lit up, under an unusual light.

I must admit, you were a perfect couple
Soothing my eyes, scorching my eyes

Heading home I told myself: I wish them well!
Now I sleep at night in a ground floor room
Making my bed on the floor, moonlight streaming in
My younger sister disappeared down a dark and winding alley

I don't know who she lives with anymore
If she's with someone today, what about tomorrow?
I'm the local sewing mistress now, the future's bleak
But the fire, Benimadhob, where's the spark ?
How about me also getting a bit spoilt ?

Translation by Carolyn Brown

Victorious

Joy Goswami

I'd traveled just one year after crossing forty when, without
warning, Extinction, holding a black staff, appeared
And said: From now on you'll live only with your body.

You'll wander around, smile sweetly, play jokes,
Babble at the office, put on a crown, turning left
and right so the light shines on your face just so.

But from now on Fire will no longer be with you.
He dwells now in the Land of Melancholy,
spiritless. He no longer has any spark.

On one side of Extinction are vast waters. On the other,
A scorched desert.
A raven is perched on Extinction's head.

Its he who is the outgoing flame
But there's still
So much writing left, I said. I need
to talk with Fire. Where is he?
Over there, Extinction said.

Extinction's finger points toward a mountain
Melancholy Mountain.

Down below Fire sits in a cave, chin resting on his fist.

Grass has grown over his shoes, up to his thighs. Roots dangle
from the muscles of his broad back and arms. Prickly vines
are snagged in his hair and beard. His gaze is empty.
No use trying to talk with him.

As I come out, I see Extinction waiting like a sentry,
Holding a black staff. The ocean is on one side. On the other,
a wasteland. He wears a white knee-length loincloth.
The raven is perched on his shaved head.
Hand over your pen, he said, and go away.

But they don't recognize the poet. That stone raven.
I snatch it from the head-top and place
A live cuckoo instead.

Now, let's see your next move

Then the inevitable happened. As the cuckoo
called out, flapping its wings twice
From Extinction's feet up to his head
Springtime burst into flames.

It spun round and round like a madman
With heart-rending cries of delight. And
With a groan, thrusting himself out of the mountain peak,

Fire stood tall, hands on his hips, and started
Rocking back and forth, toppling the peak into the water
Then a mermaid floated up, sailing her slender
craft to shore—she's racing through the sand,

a desert woman covered with a white veil ... and that's
how I left them—let them do what they like—but
after perching on my head for a long time,
writing is beating its wings, it's ready
to go with me now, back to the cave ...

Translation by Carolyn Brown

The Future Missing Girl

Joy Goswami

What has the girl discovered?
"Uncle" Raju is her mother's lover.
What has the girl overheard?

Her mother's cries of passion.
What has the girl acquired? a birthday?
Tight pants, favorite dish, a cousin's leer.

She's searched her class notes, "suggestions"
She's labored through a mountain of books
Exams, she's facing exams—studying night and day—

The other room is dark.
In the dark she's heard muffled fighting, tooth and nail
Her mother and father tearing each other apart.

Translation by Carolyn Brown

Hawk Of Iron, For You

Joy Goswami

This won't break my trance, hawk of iron, no matter
How much, boring a hole in my skull you thrust your beak in
Set your two feet on my two shoulders, your taloned
Feet, my dream won't break hawk of iron, my
Eyes are no longer in your grip, my fingers, my
Bones, my backbone are in your grip, my
Getting up and sitting down, blowing my nose,
Letting out hiccups, are in your grip,
My bolster, my pillow, my plate and glass
My clothes, my doors and windows, my fanfares, my
                              Kitchen are in your grip, but
My mind as gone from particle to a smaller particle, it
Has taken on the speed of light what can you do to
                        It hawk of iron, no matter how much,
Boring a hole in my skull you put your beak in
                        You'll find no fluid in the brain
                    Solid, black, hot
Your beak will fail, twisted, dented, hawk of iron, in your
Interior a thousand machines clang clank, a
                        Thousand televisions jingle jangle,
A thousand aeroplanes shriek swooping up and down,
                            Collision, compensation
Handshakes, killing and spy- running but what
Can your pepper-and- salt spies, your boy-faced
                  Spies do to me hawk of iron, before me
Now in a sea of fire climbs a fog of fire drops, the sun
Floats by, the sun drops, a dead star, and
Through a gap in this ocean made of countless

Suns, I slip out, I reveal myself
                Through its other mouth
Where before me is a colossal heart with all
Its pulsations,
           My eye like a transporter
Lands in it… sends signals, sends signals
      Ah, distant
        Most distant signals
       Pre- birth signals
          Envelope me…

Meanwhile you, hawk of iron, you can do as you wish
With this body of mine, I don't care anymore!

Translation by Probir Ghose

Rope

Dhiman Chakrabarty

Suicides being so common these days, it's obvious
That ropes are no longer mistaken to be snakes. But some
must think them garlands with scent of tuberose or roses.
Here's how it goes – office workers at their desks, grow tired
Pushing and pouring over ledgers and files day after day.
When fed up enough, they think of death day after day
Till suddenly one day, staring at the clothes-line,
Suicide comes to mind. I've questioned some people and found
The bell-rope in trams and buses makes them feel the same way
Others grow tired keeping count of skulls. With death
Ever on their minds, petticoat strings, waiters' belts, horses'
Tails build an obsession about suicide. Before our eyes
Suicide ropes shimmer like moonlight. And then

Every year the rains come, the ropes gather mildew
Next year it rains again, the ropes mildew again
That year it rains like earlier years, mildew again

Not a bit of rope left then for suicide, it's all rotten.

Translation by Madhuchhanda Karlekar

Doleful

Dhiman Chakrabarty

Doleful awakes early and eats, reads newspaper,
Shaves with a shiny blade; a haircut now and then-
Doleful loves wearing burnt leaf green.
Parks, restaurants, races, pros-quarters are his
favourite scene. He roams the streets all day,
Befriends strangers, chats and jokes over tea.
Back home at night he has dinner and then
Pisses in circles on the wall like a child,
Returns, lifts bedcover and sleeps with wife.
So he ages, gets heart tremors or blood sugar.
To recover his vitality Doleful now
Takes a rest-cure at some mountain resort,
Back again to finish his work at office,
And see his happy family. Call friends over
For meat, rossogolla, icecream or some beer,
And he sings on and on –
Hachi-boom, hachi-bam, kha......kha......kha......

Then men start distrusting each other again,
Blood is spilt, poison gas flies through the manhole
Quite a few workers die. A memorial service is held.
Slowly all the charm drains from Doleful's face,
His nails rot and fall. His jaw and backbone crumple.
Doleful loses heart. He realises how much he has aged.
One night, without telling a soul, he dies of a sudden.

And then another kind of Dolefulness is born amongst us.

Translation by Madhuchhanda Karlekar

Arms

Dhiman Chakrabarty

He incited the angry mob to arson, with arms upraised.
He urged the State to fire on a secret meeting, arms upraised.
As the population grew he advised felling forests to build new housing, proud arms upraised. Then he went along
On a Save The Trees campaign shouting slogans, arms upraised.
So he proceeds arms upraised, chewing paan, arms up again
Juice trickling from discoloured lips, arms up at all events.

One day he supports a plan to encircle the city with villages,
Arms upraised. Air attack within two hours, military propaganda,
Combing operations etcetera, he is all for it, arms upraised.
Comes home and falls asleep. Dreams the revolutionaries and State
In separate meetings propose the traitors' arms be chopped, he
Tries to express his views, arms upraised. Pouring sweat. Tears
Pouring like sweat. But much as he searches, cannot find his arms. He wakes, sits up.
Right hand looks for left arm, left for right, and finds the empty sleeves of his night-shirt staring at him as they flip-flap.

Translation by Madhuchhanda Karlekar

Fornication

Punnyasloke Dasgupta

The angel was flying high above:

Heat of fire, rage of packed ice
He was tired of seeing all these.

Light nerveless pressure high above
Ten young women are drawing a sledge with rattling sound
Enjoyment, fixity of rules are torn asunder
Beware young woman; this fornication is not succulent.

Going down at dead of night with mouth on a silver bowl
Wine will trickle down the cheek and chin to the navel
Ah, can the body bear the restless rambles of the whole day?

This drinking to one's health is full of possibilities, oh, flying is fun
Sleeping on watery bed, drinking dreams with eyes shut, ah...

The sledge car was rolling down
The bucolic scented bath, full of sensuousness, was rippling up all around
Give me the smile of gratifying lips, slave of cheap desire, I have stretched out my hands.

Translation by Susnata Gangopadhyay

Cunning

Punnyasloke Dasgupta

When the night suddenly chases me with raised serpent hood
The sly young woman feels a tug at her feet and moves away
Only her sound plays there in the wind
The bell-metal fairy dances and freezes in fright.
How does the lifeless thing understand everything?
Whose hood is this, since when has he raised this whip?
Can somebody explain? When will the rage subside?

This body of the hood is the garment of a snakeskin.

Translation by Susnata Gangopadhyay

Love

Punnyasloke Dasgupta

Let my heart burn in gentle heat, in the chill of the flower garden
I can take in my chest the warm glow for the sake of a woman
Let the cyclone's whirling winds come, and the sharp teeth
Boil for me white rice as sweet as flowers.

Translation by Susnata Gangopadhyay

The Blindness After Sunset

Mridul Dasgupta

I walk the path of blind after sunset ..
                While you shed silent tears,
Your book is a wonder, so thinking I call a thousand pupils in dream
While the teacher dozes, they readily play truant to
                the distant horizon

And mind you, they return, with logs of wood on their head,
                water – bag on their back
As if language is a cultivation,
And yet tell me woman what more will satiate you ?

                              Translation by Deepa Mukhopadhyay

Woman Thy Name Is Desire

Mridul Dasgupta

As a woman named hunger arrives with words of love
Who wouldn't hurl towards night, especially me a night – farer
No indecent words, yet she stole an amorous glance,
        As I drew her in my arms, unsure and anxious
Oh, what an amazing picture! As if a very rich girl had
        Left her father's home and property and come here bare and stark

Translation by Deepa Mukhopadhyay

Mishap

Mridul Dasgupta

Why these tears in the darkness of night,
Desire is the inevitable fruit of love
If I speak of religion ..more volumes, more mishaps
Have seen the blood of flowers.. having drunk that even
                                       some have easy nights
Don't you also float on the waves with child on your lap?

Soaring in the pale sky of this impoverished country
               I felt God's responsibility was surely the most;
So there are words, secret knowledge, books for your realisation

You are just a receptacle of simplicity, but think
If arithmatic of steel decorates a different garden!

Translation by Deepa Mukhopadhyay

Solution In Simplicity

Mridul Dasgupta

Solution will only be in simplicity –
                How did the cascading spring enter?
Should I speak of the deep wound, you call it indulgence

The sudden fountainhead of mist
The collected water beneath the secret grass was my discovery
You know all of it is not just rain water
                Will you then stay silent, or
Will you at last mail destiny's very own recipe
Sent late, still I shall hang it out in the broad day-light
                And listen
I too have a strange light to offer, my very own!

Translation by Deepa Mukhopadhyay

Gandhi

Subodh Sarkar

Sitting or standing?
Should Gandhi sit or stand?
He was made to sit.
Seeing that in the half light of the night
An expert said
This won't do,
For Gandhi seems to be squatting on a potty
Make him stand up, give him a stick to hold
But mere standing isn't all—
What place what's the occasion?
Whether one is begging or giving alms
Can well be made out
From the way one stands.

Pupul Jaykar said,
Gandhi crossing a bamboo- bridge
During the Noakhali riot
Catch that rare pose
It was done.

In Calcutta we say,
"There's many a slip between the cup and the lip."
In Delhi they say,
"Sheer catching isn't enough, dear,
Catch and bury."

Gandhi, tied with ropes, is unloaded from the truck.
First near the India Gate.

Hundreds burst into protest,
Not here
Gandhi is carried towards Rajghat.
No, not even here—
Great controversy sparked off
From Rajghat the truck moved towards Jumna via Tinmurti.

Gandhiji stood on the Jumna in the soft light of the dusk
He looked thinner.
"Can't you offer me room for standing anywhere?"—
He murmured
He took two steps to the left
Three to the right, tapped his stick to the ground
And then moved on straight away from the Jumna
Along the dark Indian sub-continent.—-

Translation by Kalyan Dasgupta

Sari

Subodh Sarkar

She got fifty-one saris as marriage gifts
Six more on her return for astomangala
She never saw so many saris together

She set all the blue saris on the first shelf of the almirah
Hugging a light blue one said
You are my sky
She put all the rosy ones on the second
Clasping one of them said
I call you vanity
The three peacock-blues on the third shelf
Seemed to be joy rushing in from three sides
She called the light-brown one melancholy
She got saris only as gifts through out the year
How to wear so many in one life she wondered.

But it took not even a year for that event to crack
One early evening she accompanied her
Husband to eat out chinese food
Three masked youths came and stood before them
A twelve-inch knife drove into the husband's
Lower belly cutting an "L"
Steaming hot chilly fish lay abandoned in the plate
This is politics commented the local folk.

She got fifty-one saris on her wedding
Six more on her return for astamangala

One noon when her mother-in-law was asleep
She took out all the saris and sent them
Flying from the seventh-floor balcony
Towards the world below
The mother-in-law made her wear a whitesheet of cloth
A girl only nineteen, left alone.

But that white sheet was also taken off by the three
At the local crossing
A freshly widowed girl, stripped naked, ran
Crying, help, help!
The three followed her with shrieks of wild delight'
The local folk stood speechless.
She got fifty-one saris as wedding-gifts.

Translation by Kalyan Dasgupta

How To Be A Good Communist

Subodh Sarkar

Take a morning walk on the grass, bare-foot
Sit awhile by your old mother, in the descending darkness of the evening
Throw the sickle into the air for sometime
The hammer into the river-bed
Let the stars return to the stars.

Listen to the birds
Your left side is lost
Listening to the endless slogans.
Speak softly
Good words can be uttered in low voice too.

You needn't think of the masses
Look after your own ward, rather
Rear him up well.

Translation by Kalyan Dasgupta

The Kind Of Wife We Want

Subodh Sarkar

Oh, that's a story indeed
Of the land evergreen!

We want our wife to be
An earthen pitcher with a butterfly painted thereon,
Overturning which all sins can be covered
Overnight.
She should be as youthful as
The tip of a gourd-creeper
Growing in rain
But must run away straight
From an approaching lewd.

She should serve rice
Wash the clothing
Brush the shoes
But we don't want her to betray her lust.

She'll wear vermilion
Draw designs on the floor
Prepare rice-porridge
Should keep waiting for her drunken husband
Holding the window- bar.

Oh, that's a story indeed
Of the land evergreen!
We are drunk,
Bent like a bow

We are sinners,
We return home
In a police friend's jeep
After breaking the bottle of liquor
And selling the wrist – watch off.

But getting home
We must see
Designs on the floor
And her,
Waiting alone as on marriage night
With the food served.

Translation by Kalyan Dasgupta

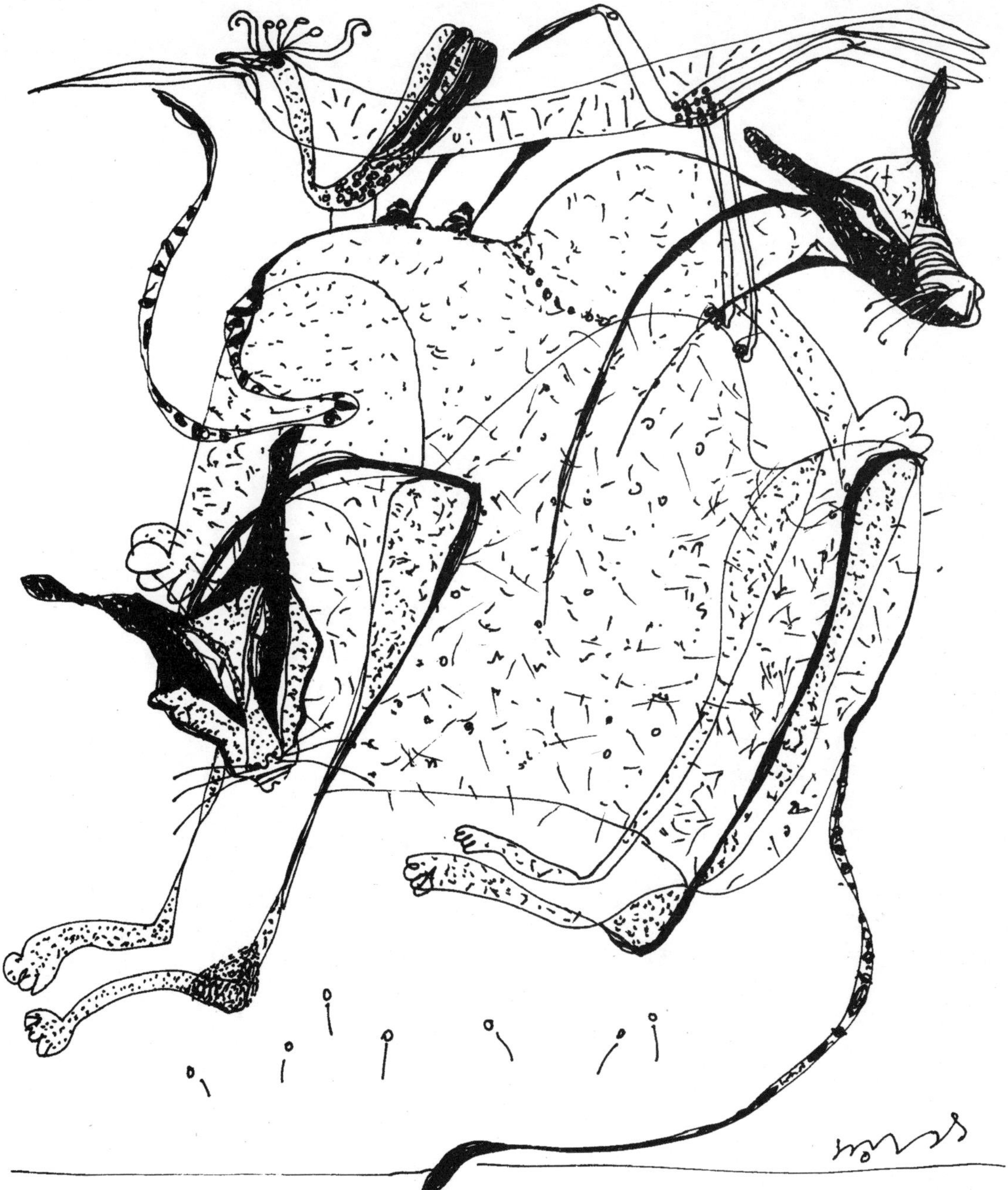

Pill

Sanjukta Bandopadhyay

Have such a depression pill whose effects you know only too well.

In the mellow twilight the head lolling slowly to the shoulder beside
Half - closed sleepy eyes; images of Maidan fleeting past
Clouds, trees—breathlessness, cramp in the abdomen
All assorted items reel inside the head
Melancholy trudges home like a dog.

Have such a sleeping pill, whose effect on dream you know only too well.

Throat choked in the evening, delirious tongue
Sleepless at midnight, watch a fairy in flight.
Broken courtyard of a temple. Two bodies beside it—-
Unfamiliar face of the flesh- and- blood goddess. The other a butcher.
The chopper poised on the pillow. Ashes fly across cremation grounds.
Night, and yet not quite night

You are returning home, with insomnia, chained like a dog

Translation by Sudeshna Banerjee

The She - Cat

Sanjukta Bandopadhyay

Without non-vegetarian food life is dull
Smell of fish-scale steeped in wings, eyebrows, pubic hair.

Holding you in my two hands, I feel
A fish playing about in water cupped in my hands.

Think you're the fog, the island,
You are the boat turning in your own fathoms,
And I, the fisherman's daughter, as if
Can't see anything— darkness all around
Rowing the boat in secret to give
Birth to a great war.

Today, like every other dinner
Fishbones lie scattered
With traces of fish still clinging.

Addicted to meat so yawning lazily
Snuggle up to your wife
Play with the ball of wool that has rolled away from her lap

Hope one day I'll gnaw and slurp into that marriage of yours
That perfect non-veg marriage of yours...

Translation by Sudeshna Banerjee

In This Birth As A Woman

Sanjukta Bandopadhyay

I love the solitude of the ladies coupe
With wool they knitted together
The expanse from the kitchen to the distant horizon of Belanagar...
From the next station those three old women— green vendors—
Will surely board the train and
Just as the helpless bespectacled skinny young lady
Comes and sits by me, I heave a sigh of relief and shift a little on my seat

At about eleven or twelve
All male species have disappeared from the vicinity—
On the adjacent ledge I see an Amazon
Crouching, bow and arrow in hand—-
Will pierce the heart if she finds one isolated.

A strange mysterious darkness all around
Awakened from sleep, I choke, breathless
No cigarettes; for a few hours now
Smokeless unpolluted atmosphere
Noon in this birth as a woman
With the spicy aroma of dal on a simmer and a feeling of security
Has crept into each crevice of the brain...

Translation by Sudeshna Banerjee

The Geometry We Could Not Learn

Sanjukta Bandopadhyay

Sakina and I
Craving to be
Two equal arms of an isosceles triangle
Had formed this faithful angle.
However far our desire to fly
However eternal the horizon, we knew
We breathed the same air, even measured the same.
Knew on the other side of the path
Lay the two faces of our inner sorrow
At a single constant point.

We hoped to construct
That uniform eternity towards which
Our legs and paths stretched
With another arm —the third arm.
I on one side and Sakina on the other
Had chosen that long straight line as our limit
One day we noticed in fright
That its complex geometrical existence had gradually tilted to a side,
While going farther down and down
It made our positions precarious——Sakina's and mine.

Two mouths still crave to whisper
Throwing to winds all formulae
But the footsteps of one are touching the confines

Of a small low room with effortless ease
And the footsteps of the other
Are gradually drawn away by the dangerous paths and the distant skies.

Translation by Sudeshna Banerjee

Apocalypse

Aneek Rudra

As our speedboat pulls away from their island
The assembled men and women
                 Wave their hands from the shore
                      Dotted with pebbles
Our boat depicts a huge shark
And the poster of the full-breasted hollywood diva arrested at her navel
How her silvery eyeliner begs lust
With fish smell
Promisory notes spilled over the village
                In the post –coital lull
With the wine we sipped from coconut-shells
Had gone into our heads, children
Saw how white froth trickled down their naked thighs
As the young dames were yet to bathe

We are leaving behind bags full of wheat
                      rajma ..edible oils
And promise to meet them again
And they presently are waiving their
     only piece of clothing in the air

How could Teresa afford to be unaware
      Of these people

And as our boat cruises along
Cigarettes light up in our hands
Lemonades pop…
The hitachi performs Robson…

Translation by Aneek Rudra

Incarnation Of Dwarf

Aneek Rudra

An excellent settlement you have guessed
Jolly people, their vanity and sentiment you have guessed
Strange tall trees and tiny grass-flowers you have guessed
In your thoughts rustling winds or a variety of
                                    small and big storms would pop up
The harpings in the deepest recess of your psyche which
                                    Would strike the chord
Slowly from the base to 'D' sharp major
Marvellous tune you have guessed
About Utopia you have guessed
Parlour of the fundamentallists you have guessed
The southern ruggedness has mesmerised you
You would bask in the glory of Espahan-Bukhara
Overwhelmed at the Gandhara art
The sculpture of Vishnu temple haunts you
Stirred you are in the corn-fields of the fertile north
Excellent turmoil you've guessed
The time of receeding shadow, you have guessed
This you, excellent by-product
Like a commodity.

Translation by Anindita Ghosh

The Portrait Of Living

Aneek Rudra

With disbelief smeared over our faces
And mathematics doppled all over
We move about alone in detours
                Occasionally walking into each other
      But for a few words exchanged
I have some acquaintances in the villages, suburbs…markets
You too are not unfamiliar with the toiling hands
Although its not that if confronted by some mortal danger
We won't mingle up with the main stream
The situation is becoming increasingly complex
            And the people more stubborn
Alien forces bent on looting our land
        Continue to divide and prosper
As if the simpleton can't see through the gestures of charity
They who play king there apparently dictating majority's destiny
They too, in truth, are only relatively free
              With so many strings attatched
Not following their statics
Eager to unleash our wrath, if we
              Jump onto some fanciful strategy
A temporary relief might be coming
But in no time the military junta
Would seize power and roughshod over the land
Was it very long ago that we had seen the
            Massacre in Indonesia?

When our feelings for the Krishna have
       Always had a back seat
And the Ganga reigns supreme

Translation by Aneek Rudra

Generation

Pinaki Thakur

The photo portrait is of my uncle. Aunty beside him.
This, my cousin brother. Prabashi Bengali settled outside Bengal.
But within India ofcourse, at Kashidham now called Benaras.
Then how Prabashi? Lets forget such quibble. Listen, my dear cousin
is a perfect tongue in Hindi, our national lingo. One day I was telling him
about Panchmundi hills, Shyamali rivers – he was also relishing like
nonsense verses... then suddenly the idiot box blurted out National programme.
An ad on detergent powder or something like that was on the screen.
in Hinglish my cousin brother called my aunt and said Had I, Mom been born from
the womb of that wife in ad, I would have been as handsome as her son there. My aunt
hung her head in shame. My goodness, if somebody changes your or my mother and
suppose replaces her even by film actress Hema, oh no, Can you imagine?
Well, you write poetry, have a go with this one.....

Translation by Boudhayan Mukhopadhyay

Girl-Friend Dear
(Make me immortal with a kiss)

Pinaki Thakur

On my birthday you gifted me
Bani Basu's novel 'Attaining twenty-first'
But I have crossed my twenty-one
Years ago, not today, not now.

The backdrop is noisy .Poverty. Grievence
Tears. Curses. Disgusting.
Where will I go today? Let me go to the market place
Thousands of people are going that way.

I'm friendless in this city, only you were my girl-friend dear
But I lost you for I wasn't rich. Astrologer warned,

'Your Mercury and Sun are ominous. Beware'. 'What will I do then, Sir?'
'Let the year end' .. a consolation
The twenty —one year old guy cared two hoots about Mercury, Venus or Jupiter.

Do you still do the ritual days ?Abstinenace, fasting, et al?
Does your mind still quiver in tension if I return late?

What book did you gift on my birthday? Bani Basu's 'Attaining twenty-first'
You never kissed me. Always said 'No' always said 'not today'

Snatching is the rule for survival in your world. Brute force is Free Will
Entering twenty-first my jaws broke. Retaliate blow by blow.

Brute force means Free Will
Brute force means, Free Will?

Translation by Boudhayan Mukhopadhyay

Passenger

Pinaki Thakur

Blue school building. Ivy - creepers.
Morn. Music tutor Srabani sister is nice. Srabani Biswas
Double M.A. (T.V, Radio famed) over there her credentials
written on the board. Classes on classical music are held regularly here
Tabla, Esraj and modern songs. Dance katthak. Tha tha thei

Somewhat uneven broken road bends. First bus to Dhannyakuria
Jolts to a halt. 'Ladies hold the stop, eh?' she briskly came out,
Is she Srabani Biswas? May be. A bit intimidating, serious looking
Music teacher takes her class in prose? the bus starts with a shudder.

Trunks, suitcase. Sackful of potatoes too. The darkish girl in bridal dress
'Have your tea, snacks or whatever at the next stop, Kansona village..'
Election posters. The shopkeepers home and hearth black in coal fumes
Van Gogh used to come and paint here dewdrops on sunflower.

Palash flowers turn scarlet. But fails to impress.
None to put them on hair-buns. The song mistress is absent
The morning student practises his wonder with the sky

Translation by Boudhayan Mukhopadhyay

Signal

Jahar Sen Majumdar

A homely custard-apple tree. Below it
On a hammock, the evening swings.
Sanatorium near by. Where consumptives live.
All under the treatment of a harmless green snake.
Yellow leaves keep falling. Knowing to be endless
Falling on and on gives them deep happiness.

My coming here has one advantage. The open window
Gives a view of the sanatorium opposite. Sometimes
With cycle bell ringing and stethoscope round it's neck
The green snake arrives. Leaning against the yellow trunk
He keeps telling me of such strange happenings.
My parents were his patients. Not only that,
For thousands of years all my numerous relatives have
Been coming to him for help at one time or other. Am I too
Becoming a consumptive? The green snake
Reassures me. He says that in the last three months
I've been transformed thrice. Strange. I was first
An earwig. Then a worm. Then a naked
Squirrel. What then? What am I now, really?
The green snake gives a sly grin and rides off
Ringing his cycle bell.

I sit in silence at the open window. And outside I see
Amid fistfuls of moonlight, green snakes hanging
All over the sky. And through the wide universe
The constant ringing of a cycle bell.

Translation by Madhuchhanda Karlekar

Ladder

Jahar Sen Majumdar

I saw an ochre coloured youth sitting
on a tree-stump quietly reading a book
page after page. What was he reading? I
stood behind him and peeped. There was
nothing on any page, not a single letter.

I saw an ochre-coloured youth. He had
No eyes. He sat on a tree-stump
With an owl like a black pupil
On his lap. He was kissing the owl
Now and then. I went up and asked,
Can you see nothing at all? He said,
Yes, I see the world through the eyes
Of this owl.

Who, who, who was this youth ? You must
Be dying to know. But I shan't tell,
Never reveal his identity. Only
When black clouds gather in the sky,
Deep black clouds, down whose ladders
The moonlight shall descend in a myriad
Snaky spirals, on that very night
You shall see from your rooms an ochre
Coloured youth moving in circles round all
Your homes. And from his throat you'll
Hear a muffled groaning.

Translation by Madhuchhanda Karlekar

Back Of One's Head

Jahar Sen Majumdar

As I laid my head on the pillow, something strange happened.
I saw a gap in its centre, and a narrow lane
Running through far far into a fading distance
I was going down that lane, further into the organised
Depth. So many countless things lay along the way
There it was, a blue hospital. Large black ants
Were hospitalized there. Spotted sleepy spiders
Making envelopes out of a slope. Snakes playing
On pipes. Stale blood spilt from wombs. A little
Further on, a delivery room built on slime. Feet
Flying in thousands. Feet bordered with red dye.
A tiny sapling played up like a tabor. New paws
New wedding cards. Birthing pretty-poverty and
Needy-navvy. Ribs of a dark world. Students. Lantern
Letters. Red and blue tiles set on a cow's back.
I creep forward through the crevice in my pillow,
I want to come back, I can't, want to stop, I can't,
Kids aim iron balls at my half-woken spine.

To whom shall I show this strange world within my pillow
I wonder. And above all, it is dead men who wish
To write of the mysterious life within the pillow.
The dead who too kept their heads on pillows, but
Couldn't see the strange secret lane.

Translation by Madhuchhanda Karlekar

Open Letter To Freud

Mallika Sengupta

An extra limb in man's body
Has eternal power, earth's ownership
According to Mr. Freud for want of it woman is inferior
As an underling she envies man's virility

Nature is uncaring
Man is uncaring
Children are uncaring
Only Freud cares for women!

Who cares for compassion! Chitrangada? Joan of Arc?
Simone De Beauvoir or dark Draupadi!

"Penis -envy" is a term
Coined by Mr. Freud
That extra which only man possesses
That's what diminishes a woman
So she is uncertain in childhood
Decorates the Shivalinga with flowers at girlhood
Her playroom is full of dolls and utensils
For it's said that she is her mother's replica.

Whereas Rohit rehearses for war
American soldiers in jungle fatigues in his room
Machine guns fusillade tra-ra-ra
As man's aggressiveness grows in him
If he claws cheeks with sharp nails
Man child's extra prowess makes grandmothers beam

That extra bit in his body, that's the license
Which will make him the world's owner.

Rohit will be the owner of which world?
Where Rohita will be his partner! Inferior sex!
On galloping horseback with drawn sword
Emperor Rohit will set to conquer the world
And he will be decked for war by mother, sister, wife
That is just what you wanted Mr. Freud!
If a woman warrior arrives from the opposite side
Will he abandon arms like Bhishma
"I will not take up arms against women"
Implying I'll not allow woman right to arms

This is primal man's sexual politics
Freud, because you belong to the extra limb group
You assume women are inferior and hence envious!

During my childhood I felt no penis-envy
My self-identity was complete
Even today I'm a confident, complete woman,
A sensitive dark girl of the Third World

Shall stand against you from today
Who is inferior who is superior which is more or what is less
Who has given you the duty of solving
All these complex issues, Mr. Freud!!

Translation by Sanjukta Dasgupta

Tell Us Marx

Mallika Sengupta

She spun rhymes, wove blankets
The Dravidian woman who sowed wheat
In the Aryan man's fields, reared his kids
If she isn't a worker, then what is work?

Tell us Marx, who is a worker who isn't
New industrial workers with monthly wages
Are they the only ones who work
Slum life is the Industrial Age's gift
To the worker's housewife
She draws water, mops floors, cooks food
After the daily grind, at night
She beats her son and weeps
She too isn't a worker?
Then tell us marx, what is work!

Since housework is unpaid labour, will women simply
Sit at home and cook for the revolutionary
And comrade he is alone who wields hammer and sickle!
Such injustice does not become You

If ever there's a revolution
There will be heaven on earth
Classless, stateless, in that enlightened world
Tell us Marx
Will women then become the handmaidens of revolution?

Translation by Sanjukta Dasgupta

A Mark Of Blood

Mallika Sengupta

Man, I have never raised my hand against you

The first time you marked my forehead with blood
I felt pain, but I didn't say so to you, I didn't.

The dry soil doesn't yield blooming roses the peacock doesn't dance
Yet for ages have we dug the shores for drinking water
Child in arms we have seen glow worms and pointed out the Orion.

We know very well that the earth is a woman, the sky a primitive man,
Then why have you enshackled my hands in chains
And for a thousand years prevented me from seeing the sun?

Don't humiliate the earth on which you stand
Man, I have never raised a hand against you.

Translation by Malabika Sarkar

A Fish Whip In The Feudal Age

Mallika Sengupta

In my previous birth I was a slave woman's daughter
We had no room of our own, drew comfort from the hay
While next door lived the precious cattle
Mother disappeared in the middle of the night

Nobody knew where she went, why she wept at night
Nobody knew why I didn't have enough to eat!

At thirteen my master slung me across a wooden stick
In the middle of the market place
Prodded the fish with a whip, the cloth was removed
Leaving the body bare, lifting the gill flap to check
The health and robustness.

I have no shame and am not supposed to feel fear
The fish that is a whip today lived in the river Kaljani

Translation by Malabika Sarkar

By My Personal Memorial

Prabal Kumar Basu

The way I am living, my persisting ways of surviving will make me
a State someday. Diplomats will represent me in
the Non-Aligned summit. The name of the Prime Minister of this State is index finger.
The thumb is his personal secretary. The working president of the ruling party is the
ring finger ...
An ornament, inert and ineffective.

My ankles are thickened with dirt, the skin wrinkled around
My elbows and knees. Dark. The backward class's colony. My libido after a long
crusade in demand for a separate state or country in the guise of some religious or
linguistic uprising has become exhausted and limp. So many days, I've forgotten the
taste of a kiss ...... my lips are almost icy white .. people call it Kashmir.

The way of my life will genuinely make me a State some day. Within the retina of my
two eyes will keep awake some mindless blind like Lok Sabha and Rajya Sabha. Lakhs of
votes in hordes will race towards them from the nose and ears.

In the rib cage the revolution will hibernate as rusted bars in the jails

This State is called India.
The separatists lurk in its nooks and corners. The starved unfold like pores all over the
expanse of the body.

I feel no compassion for them. I do not have any sympathy for them. I am seasoned
living togather with them.

My way of existing, one day will make
Me India. Nobody's going to point out

......That guy
......The young poet
No one will propose .. let us organise a poets' conference
This country India, as if, is my memorial. Personal.
So long I am lying by its side .... as a dialogue, as a story, a song and as a memory above all .... Oblivious to all
Only a few friends sometimes call out, discreetly ......Prabal, Prabal ......

Translation by Barnali Roy

Living Scape

Prabal Kumar Basu

Some days at the market
I end up buying myself
Measured on a set of scales
So the weight's not even a hair short.
Then I march home
Proudly with my bulging bag.
I set down the shopping bag and say
to my wife, 'Look what I've brought you:
A head for braising, a spine to stir fry
with vegetables, and the rest for korma.'
My wife spends the whole day cooking me
While I'm absorbed in the newspaper ...
inflation, market shares, new import policy
As mouth-watering smells drift from the kitchen
I grow four times as hungry to eat myself.

We sit down together to eat me in the afternoon.
Finished, we belch with satisfaction.
Then I dig into myself again,
Intoxicated by my feasting.

By evening I begin to feel sick
My belches star to stink.
Symptoms of indigestion become apparent—I'm amazed
to see that while others have digested me
Easy as pie, inside my own self
I can't digest myself at all.

Some days at the market I see
a man just like me
skinning me, getting me ready for sale.

Translation by Carolyn Brown

Rhino

Prabal Kumar Basu

A rhino had been hiding in a file.
It jumped out one day when the file
was opened and sat down on all
the office chairs, one by one.

One day at the office I saw
A rhino, seated on my regular chair.
I almost choked, then noticed
How much he looked like me,
Pouring over my papers intently.

Panicking, I rush to the boss's chamber—
There's another rhino, looking just like
the boss, swivelling in his chair.
In the boss's antechamber I'm astonished
to see another rhino-alike of Ms. Sanyal, boss's secretary
Surrounded by rhinos, I'm baffled:
Has the office turned into a sanctuary?

Back home, what's this I see?
An exact replica of my wife, a rhino fixing tea.
Terrified, I wonder, must I from now on be
a poacher hiding in their preserve?
Beneath the thick layers of skin
I can't recognize the actual people at all.

Translation by Carolyn Brown

The Wall

Prabal Kumar Basu

It's taken me a long time to realize that a wall
has been accompanying me from the very start
and that I've been talking ever since ... to a wall.

I can see marshes from afar, gold-spiked fields,
but when I go near, a mossy wall obscures everything.
Awakening, I realize I've spent the night with the wall.
The wall fences in my room and makes it cramped.
I've often imagined jumping over it, I've even taken the leap,
but the wall has always resurfaced and stood by me an embodiment of indifference.

After a long journey when my back touched the wall
I realized it was there from the start,
And, because it has accepted our good and bad alike,
Even though each of us is a separate individual,
We can lean on the wall and spin in place.

Translation by Carolyn Brown

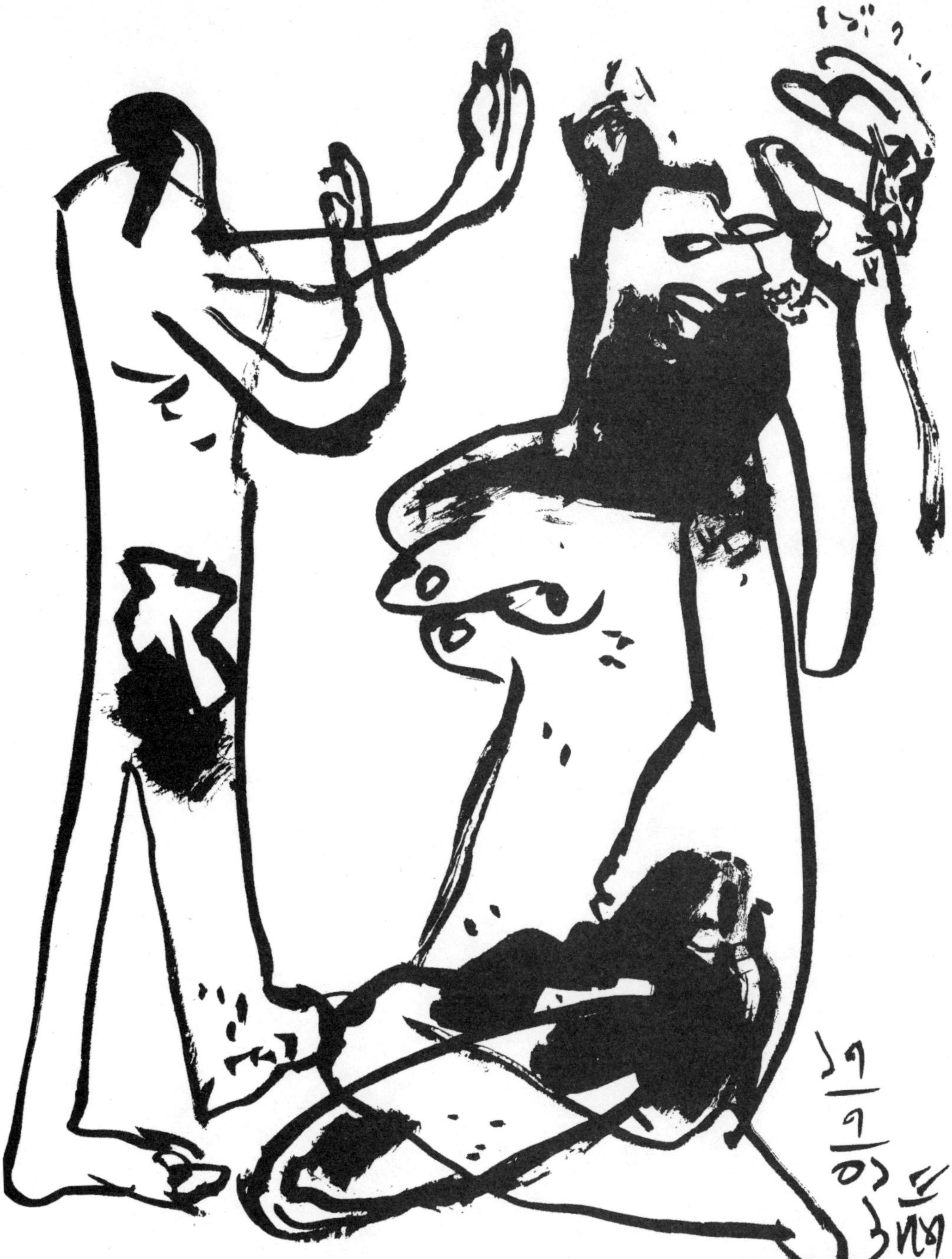

India: A Search

Joydev Basu

I have come to Ayodhya after many years for a particular reason, my lord-
I've come to look for my mother's birthplace.
 No, I don't know my religion,
I don't know who my father was
Neither did my mother.

My mother Munnabai was born here in a shanty
My grandmother couldn't tell for certain who fathered her
And so the question of class and caste doesn't arise at all,
My mother only knew who her mother was, my lord,
Consider whether this could be called a matriarchal family,
Though what the word 'family' means is not clear to me
Rather, listen- what I saw
Before I boarded the train without a ticket when I was a child.

I don't remember clearly, but that arid, dark
Unsanitized cramped shanty,
Beggars, tricksters, former convicts, drunkards...and
In the dead of some nights a sudden whistle...
The dead-drunk pot-bellied constable breaking into our room...
Smell of alcohol in his breath... lecherous smile on his betel-stained mouth...
My mother pushing me out - that night,
The night of countless stars, the night of golden halogens
I'd spend propping myself against a roadside wall.
I could tell from experience
How many days from then mother would start retching again...

That's it. What I did after I left Ayodhya
Is not relevant here. My lord,
I had only heard that my mother was able to reach to the brickhouse from the shanty
And then even the sheeshmahal before youth left her
And then, life kicked her all the way back to the shanty
Where she died.

Forgive me if my eyes turn moist,
But so many years later, searching for my mother's birthplace,
What do I see?
Some are saying - a mythical king was born here.
Some are saying - a badshah driven from the middle East came here.
I don't know if any mythical character
Can possibly be born.
I don't know whether the footsteps of the general who came here so long ago
Can still be seen clearly.
But I know that my mother was born here— here
Because I was born here too.

I am not scared of death, I don't crave for a birth in the heaven
I am not enticed by Mandar or amrit.
Only for this shanty of mine - my roza is for my birthplace—my fasting

Prayer through the eight praharas— and namaz five times a day
My lord,
Have pity, return my motherland to me.
Return it to me before I turn desperate.

Translation by Sudeshna Banerjee

Twenty-Seventh Birthday

Joydev Basu

Now listen, you honour us with your visit only once a year and don't bother to keep track of what's happening. In a few days the hair will start turning grey. This is the time when some paths suddenly turn smooth. The two feet just decide not to tread any road except these boulevards or avenues. This is what happens in common life; what's the use of complaining, tell me. This is the time when courage dithers. Admit it or not, termites start eating your ribs, bones; eating into the bones, marrow, intelligence, conscience. You don't have the responsibility of looking after this earth, they say. No responsibility? So did I think like a fool that I too am fated to have the light! Ok then. That's that. I won't say anything to anybody. Just sit quietly waiting for you and watch the leaves fall one by one. And some year when you come, children will raise their eyebrows and shrug like a sahab pretending surprise. What will you do that year? Will you go back, never to return again?

Translation by Sudeshna Banerjee

Arowal Or Kansara or....

Joydev Basu

I had wanted a land of my own, and so under the dust
I stay squat, blood thickened with poison

I had wanted land to till, and the police Brahmarshi
Stuffed my throat with lead

I don't want a dismembered country and naturally
Wallowing in the aroma of fallen leaves in the mountain-forest

Been born to live, and so in Arowal or Darjeeling
The dead body means the same

The bullet creates such intimate bonding between nations
Johannesberg- Panama- Ganga

Does the heart still crave for Lenin? Tell your heart- Yes,
Tell your heart-Yes, despite everything, yes

Translation by Sudeshna Banerjee

For Comrade Musa Mollah

Joydev Basu

Do convey my regards to Winnie and Nelson and
To Jinji my comradeship.

You surely would have read that Turkish poet who writes-
India is a country of Asia, and Calcutta a city in India...
Yes I live in that Calcutta
Calcutta- from where you will return after addressing a meeting of three lakh people
You are now returning to a land of
Black blood, black sweat and blue diamonds.

If you look out from the window of a plane
You can't tell the difference between this country and that.
If you stand, looking out into a dry field
There is not much difference.
You have seen both ways, so
I can understand your emotion as you
Return from the gathering of three lakh people.
No there is nothing much to worry about Reagan
Because he is at once of Contra and Africana
Not an American.

You see, words yield more words, you don't have too much time on your hands
And I had very little to say.
This meeting has conveyed to the people of your country all that was to be conveyed
Our leaders have contacted your leaders and surely
Robert Mugabe has known by now
That we have done
Everything that needed to raise Botha's blood pressure.

Only on my behalf
On behalf of a third grade poet from Calcutta
Convey my regards to Winnie and Nelson, and
Comradeship to Jinji.

Translation by Sudeshna Banerjee

Poem of 12 noon

Rahul Purakayastha

You poster girl besides the colourful tent
Femme fatale, eyes emitting danger
Tresspassing you means ultra-modernity

Brownish mole on your breast, all your suspicions
Embolden me, I creep reptile–like, even in open market

Your wish urges me in that direction
The sky of the tent is torn, you beside it, oh woman

Give me too some shade, moon, give hunger, your insomnia

Translation by Boudhayan Mukhopadhyay

Open Jaws

Rahul Purakayastha

A huge open- jawed mouth is chasing me, its maya and civilization
Chasing me, its degradation and moans
Chasing me....

And yet I longed for exuberence, yes exuberence
I wanted greyness, wanted to mingle
Simply mingle with it completely

As for writing, I never wanted to write anything ever
Never wished deeply to befriend strangers

Wanted your support, you too, never preferred
To flee, wanted you to be with me a bit longer, only you

You open mouth, our self- indulgence
I think witty tongue also irritates you...

Turmoil amnesia-loving, soft light and shade

Translation by Boudhayan Mukhopadhyay

Mask

Rahul Purakayastha

A monster face, knowing it a mask
For chhou-dance, I brought it from Purulia

Now at dusk when blind Gods
Tread on air, this face smiles

Lost in happiness, after blissful union
Creeps up the rooms wall

When the wavy light of candle falls
On its eyes, the face seems familiar

The one I had evaded with morbid taunts
Seeks my provocation now

Translation by Boudhayan Mukhopadhyay

Twenty-Fifth Baisakh

Rupak Chakrabarty

I was then asleep beside my father
Nobody woke me up
My father was having high fever
My mother while bathing his head was softly singing,
"Alone I launch my singing boat ..."
How did she know ! I was then small
I was then asleep
That afternoon, my father passed away while turning on his side
Only his lips were quivering as he uttered,
"Oh thou touchstone of purifying fire .. "
My father was a KGB member
My father was a CPI member
After the last rites I poured over the first volume of Gitabitan
And song number 212 at page ninetyfour was missing

There were people thronging everywhere, the court-yard, the verandah
As the procession started on its journey
It was Sisir uncle, who asked all, not to utter prayers
Then who was it, was it my mother?
She pressed that page with song number 212 into the
Cold hand of my father, and said
I have no god of my own Tagore
Will you please take care of him ?

Translation by Deepa Mukhopadhyay

Fish

Rupak Chakrabarty

Kamini aunty, that little woman
Sat under the palmbush
Infront of Hiranbala school
Her day's work was done. Ours too
She sat in the mid-summer noon, unmindful
With far away look in her eyes
Do you remember aunt, that man who was your husband just for a day
Ditched you, never returned and your maiden name gone
You never saw his face and yet for his sake you never had fish
Thinking him dead
The other day mother sent me to the market
To buy fish, yes, just for you
At that moment, with the smell of hilsa all around
The name came from your village
The man for whom you hadn't touched fish for fourteen years
Actually died two days back
Mother wept a lot, pleaded, even insisted
But you didn't touch the fish, not even the gravy

Infront of Hiranbala school
Under the palmbush sat
Kamini aunty, that little woman
Why, why Kamini aunty, why didn't you
Drift away someday with a fish
To some faraway river mouth!

Translation by Deepa Mukhopadhyay

The White Letter

Rupak Chakrabarty

To
The Editor Sir,
My poems which you discarded as worthless
Excluded me from the circle of those elite poets since
Things were not upto the mark
Those same poets have came to my house today
The poems you once rejected have grown into a forest
Multi-hued birds are flitting about in the depth of verdure
Respected Sir, though nothing never worked in my favour
The dawn of a new morrow has arrived for me
I wonder when these birds of light have come to
Adorn the branches of that once rejected forest of poems!
The Sun has opened the windows in the east
And now light streams in on those refused poems

With due respect I must ask for more patience
Give me light that I may learn not to utter slander
More light that I may stand before you once
Just once, holding my new poems

Translation by Deepa Mukhopadhyay

The Uncertain Path

Chiranjib Basu

The seed of solution was hidden in some friends' eyes
The blood rises, the blood falls - the sloping field - the river in the horizon
Do you hear mystic calls from the other side? Friend's ask
The river incessantly flows down to eternity.

The solution was ready in some dear friends' lips
The sound rises, the sound ebbs, scorched fields- the path faraway
Are you keen to roam on that path? Friends ask.
The path is lined with small camps of friends on either side, duels
There's a plethora of drinks, money and women in those camps
I too become a party
The unwritten verses hibernate like snakes in my body.

Translation by Barnali Roy

A Dream Originated Dialogue

Chiranjib Basu

A list of things to have faith in at this point of time

1) Darkness can be believed, as I
   Can't see behind my back
   Taking advantage of the darkness, many will try to
   Ride my ass.

2) Love! Umm plausible
Otherwise there's no point in creating a balcony
Where girls will not saunter in the evening

3) Don't make the mistake of trusting rain
The crops will wither in field after field,
We pine for rainfall
And we all know at this crossroad
Any day can't be rainy day, anyway!

4) NO ENTRY board is apparently trustworthy

We should not feel miserable
   We know after a hectic day, the board will
   Turn around in a jiffy.
   We all will then be facing an empty goalpost
   All of us proficient in the diamond shot.

Apart from the above, the factory chimney, locks, high-powered lens, the auntie next door, the first of the month, the music teacher, the red comb, condom, landscape, red dye, local councilor, Bijaya Dashami, nausea, Yash Chopra, these are not worth relying on, believe me.

Translation by Barnali Roy

Pilgrimage

Chiranjib Basu

I am not a wanderer
Nor do I believe in travelling
I sit pensively on the flower
Laying down my wings.
I am not that bee to hop from one flower to flower
I sprawl myself like the ocean, eyes closed
I do not wander from port to port
I invariably anchor myself to one.

I hide myself in one particular flower
My vision steals to possess that one particular blossom
And wait if you ever unfurl your body
Then I'll go for my pilgrimage.

Only once in life I'll stretch beyond boundaries, I promise.

Translation by Barnali Roy

The Archer

Bibhas Roychaudhury

Being flogged on and on
The Bengali language has fallen flat.
Blood on the leaves of trees, blood rubs on the flowers
The tongues of the Ganga and the Padma
Are shrouded in mist.
Bengali grass on either side...severed lips ...suppressed wailing

Who invade? Who wipe out songs and poems?
Who are brushing off the dew from the Bengali grass?
The swans of the pond? Kalmi creepers? The baul of the dawn?
We are arrows of the Bengali rhyme to resist them.

No matter if you miss the rhyme,
Never forget the tongue
A whole nation, mind you, will be wiped off
If the objective is lost
Can the guns silence the nation
Whose blood is full of songs and lips full of love-poems?
There is a master above the master.

If the Bengali language loses the fight,
Such great love will also die, alas !

The leaves sing, the flowers sing in rage.

Translation by Kalyan Dasgupta

Rice

Bibhas Roychoudhury

Lots of paddy lands are there...
Why, should we, then starve?
Is it because I'm a poet?
Why have you made friends with a poet, why?
Your horizons will be scorched...
Why did you keep loving me everyday in empty stomach?

It stormed whole night... the grace of the morn is different
Look, there comes a light, I gobble it up
You too have a part, no other food is in store today.
Letters have filled the mind, hunger comes in flocks.

You believe things will improve soon
Hunger will be appeased... the shades beneath the eyes will go
But how? More and more poems will come.
A lot more will be written...
Boat-songs instead of rice.

Writing on so many paddy fields
And the native land
I'm defeated to the rice pot, not a grain of rice anywhere.

Translation by Kalyan Dasgupta

My Dear Father

Bibhas Roychoudhury

You are a vagabond, dad. You married
and were caught in a trap.
Gone with the wind and burnt up is your
Opera - role of ladylove.
Mother gave up wearing torn frock
The partition married you off in a hurry.
You failed to have a grip on the forces of life ...
Mother didn't even accept you..
Amidst terrible rows
We, the three brothers and sisters, were born....

Rolling tree - leaf bidis all day long,
Taking frothy rice at night,
Late- night reading of the Red Book.
       Trance.
At midnight...you ... dad would
      Turn Khulna
And mother Jessore,
I visualised free Bangladesh in sleepy eyes
Long long before the radio broadcast.

You are a vagabond, dad. You fought
With your boss, would
Lose your job.
Mother was obstinate, stubborn, non-believer.
She would so often starve, but would never grumble.
Always quarrelsome, dad you left home.
Not the relation, mother knew, but hunger would bring you back.

You gave up dreaming, dad,
You turned desperate in search of food
You were deprived like an insect from
Path to path, country to country, rice to rice,
Love to love, my dad.
Yet, dad, when I compose verse
I forget all about your ways.
Yet, dad, you are what you are, just a father
And not mother by any stretch.

Translation by Kalyan Dasgupta

A Strange Affair

Mandakranta Sen

Speak to my mother and father
I don't mind
We'll talk later.

Everything is very restrained
But in secret that you are so reckless
When did I realize this?

My mother likes you quite
Father looks upon you as a brother
But you are really my friend.

Why hasn't auntie come, love?
Never ever tell her
That I can kiss so well.

In order to open the front door
Together we'll climb down the stairs
At those moments we go crazy.

Stormy breath, behind the stairs
Sudden sting of scorpion
Incessant smarting

Blood tinged: never mind
My face in your chest
Fits in so snugly

Are Auntie and Mitali keeping well?
Do they come close to you
Do they look for some sign?

I'll go to your office tomorrow
Exactly at four twenty five
Then everything will go topsy-turvy

Climbing the Shahid Minar
I'll yell to the skies
Indra uncle is my lover.

Translation by Sanjukta Dasgupta

Alone In Moon City

Mandrakranta Sen

There's such a surrendering moon in the sky
Truly, I never saw one such before
Security guards were pacing the government roads
And the moon, slipping in,
Bathed my face and neck in salty moonbeams.

There's such a devastating moon in the sky
Truly, I never saw one such rising before
The fullbodied minibuses before and behind me
Swallowing people like demons as they move
And she, ahead of me with brisk steps
Walking along and shouting: Catch me
Holding on to life I started scaling
Death's messengers one by one
That was a very dangerous sport.

When even the stout and virile minibuses
Entered the garages exhausted
The garages fell asleep
Sleep entered the underworld
I stood there like a wraith
On the snuffed out road; where from I am not aware
Salty languor slided down the neck and back

A little afar, a little higher
Even then the moon was silently dying
For a relationship.

Translation by Sanjukta Dasgupta

When Just You

Mandrakanta Sen

If I looked into someone's eyes I can tell
Whether love is possible with him
Sometimes for me

On the roads, pavements, buses, trams, in friend's homes
Sometimes my gaze penetrates
An unguarded face

I know someone among them
Will immerse me
In salty disaster

In the inevitable afternoon sprouting out of the soil
Will rise sweat drenched back
Someday

I can talk about these right now
When, just you
Stand on the staircase...

Translation by Sanjukta Dasgupta

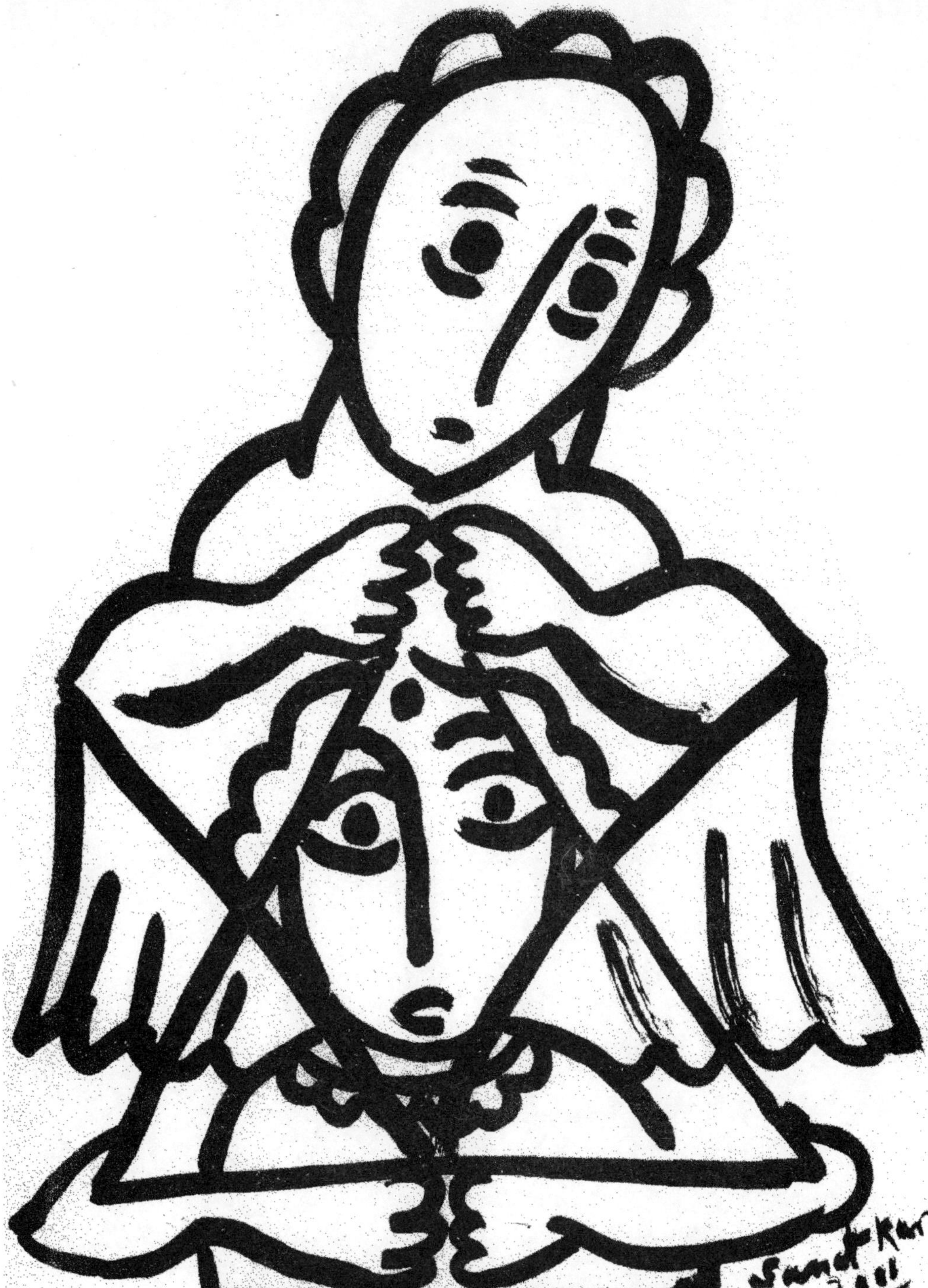
Sanat Kar
2001

THE POETS

1. **Arun Mitra** : (1909 - 2000) Born in Jessore in erstwhile undivided Bengal, now Bangladesh, obtained Ph.D in French language and literature at the Sorbonne. Taught French at France and at the Allahabad University. First volume of poetry was published in 1943. Received Akademi award in 1979 for the poetry collection *Khunjte Khunjte Eto dur* (A Long way, in quest). Translated French poetry into Bengali. Awarded D.Litt. fron Rabindra Bharati University in 1990.

2. **Subhas Mukhopadhyay** : (1919) Brought up in Rajshahi, now in Bangladesh and settled in Kolkata since 1930. A erstwhile marxist, he worked in the jute mills and the docks for organising the labour movement. Never took up a regular job for livelihood. First volume of poetry was published in 1940. Received Sahitya Akademi award for the poetry collection *Jata Durei Jai* (As far as I go) in 1964. Received Jnanpith award. Translated from *Neruda, Hikmat* and *Hafiz*. Also written travelogues and novels.

3. **Birendra Chattopadhyay** : (1920 - 1985) Born in Bikrampur, Dhaka, now Bangladesh. First volume of poetry was published in 1942. A leftist in political beliefs. He worked with Tea Estates, Banking Corporation and as a teacher in school for some time.

4. **Arun Sarkar** : (1922 - 1980) His first book was published in 1952. Edited little magazine *Kabita Patrika* for a considerable period of time.

5. **Nirendranath Chakrabarty** : (1924) Born in a small village in Bangladesh. Educated in Kolkata. His first book was published in 1954. A journalist by profession also worked as the editor of *Anandamela*, a popular children's magazine. Received Akademi award in 1974 for poetry collection *Ulanga Raja* (Naked King). He has also books on the theory of poetry.

6. **Manindra Gupta** : (1926) Born in Barishal, Bangladesh. Educated in Kolkata. First book published in 1949.

7. **Sarat Kumar Mukhopadhyay** : (1931) Born in Puri, Orissa. His first volume of poetry was published in 1957. A chartered accountant by profession and a management graduate from London. Also written short stories which have been translated into English and also included in various short story collections.

8. **Aloke Sarkar** : (1931) Born in Kolkata. His first book was published in 1952. Edited Shatavisha a noted little magazine of sixties. By profession a college teacher.

9. **Shankha Ghosh** : (1931) Born in Chandpur, now in Bangladesh. First poetry collection was published in 1956. An academic and a critic, he taught Bengali at Jadavpur University. Received Akademi award in 1977 for his collection of poetry *Babarer Prarthana* (Babar's Prayer). Received Saraswati Samman (felicitation). He was a fellow at the International writing programme at IOWA university during the sixties. Also has a number of publications of essays to his credit.

10. **Alokeranjan Dasgupta** : (1933) Born in Kolkata. First book published in 1952. Edited poetry anthology *Saptasidhu Dasdiganta*. Received Akademi award in 1992 for book *Marami Karat* (The Mystic Sow). Translated German authors in Bengali. Divides his time between Germany and Kolkata. Teaching New Indology in University of Heidelberg. His academic works include *The Lyric in Indian Poetry* (1962) and *Goethe and Tagore* (1974).

11. **Shakti Chattopadhyay** : (1933 – 1995) One of the most important poet in post Tagorean period. First book published in 1961 and has more than fifty poetry books to his credit. He received Sahitya Akademi award in 1983 for poetry book *Jete Pari Kinto Keno Jabo* (I can, but why should I go). He virtually dominated Bengali Poetry during sixties and seventies. Has also written novels and translated Kalidasa, Ghalib, Rilke, Neruda. Lived a bohemian life that once used to be the talk of the time. An early associates of Hungry movement. Worked as a journalist in *Ananda Bazar Patrika*.

12. **Sunil Gangopadhyay** : (1934) Born in Faridpur, now in Bangladesh, settled in Kolkata during forties. Edited little magazine *Krittibas,* which became the platform for young poets during the fifties and sixties. During early sixties he participated in the International writing programme at IOWA University, USA. Apart from poetry he has equally excelled in short stories, novels and in children's literature. Received Akademi award in 1985 for his novel *Sei Somai* (Those Days). His works have been widely translated into English. Works with *Ananda Bazar Patrika* as an Associate Editor.

13. **Benoy Mazumdar** : (1934) Born in Burma, first book published in 1961 before any of his poems appeared in any magazine. An engineer by qualification he used various mathematical terminology in his poems. Now a loner lives away from the city in a place called Thakurnagar.

14. **Tushar Roy** : (1934-1977) Born in Kolkata. The most bohemian poet of sixties. First book published in 1969.

15. **Samarendra Sengupta** : (1935) First book was published in 1962. An early associate of *Krittibas* later became the editor during early seventies. During early eighties published another little magazine named *Bivabh* which received wide appreciation of the critics.

16. **Amitava Dasgupta** : (1935) Born in Kolkata, first book published in 1957. Editor of prestigious little magazine *Parichay*, published since 1932. A leftist in belief is also a colomnist of a daily newspaper. Teacher of Bengali langnage in a Kolkata college.

17. **Pranabendu Dasgupta** : (1936) An early associate of *Krittibas*. First book was published during early sixties. A teacher of comparative literature in Jadavpur University also edited little magazine *Alinda*.

18. **Tarapada Roy** : (1936) Born in Tangail district of now Bangladesh and had his early education there. First book was published in 1958. He is also a popular writer of humorous anecdotes as well as a columnist. Worked with the state Government.

19. **Utpal Kumar Basu** : (1937) Born in Kolkata. First book was published in 1961. Worked with UGC.

20. **Shaktipada Brahmachari** : (1937) Borne in Sylhet, now in Bangladesh. First book was published during late sixties. Though from Assam his poems could make a distinct mark in Bengali poetry. Remained associated with little magazine *Sahitya Nabaparjaye* published from Assam.

21. **Vijaya Mukhopadhyay** : (1937) Born in Bikrampur, Dhaka, now in Bangladesh. First book was published in 1967. Did her masters in Sanskrit from Calcutta University.

22. **Manibhusan Bhattacharya** : (1938) Born in Chattagram, now in Bangladesh. First book was published in 1952. Edited an anthology of ten young poets during seventies. School teacher.

23. **Pabitra Mukhopadhyay** : (1940) Born in Barishal, now in Bangladesh. First book was published in 1960. Edited noted little magazine of sixties named Kabipatra. A college teacher.

24. **Piyush Raut** : (1941) Born in Tripura. Maintained the trend of Bengali poetry from Tripura, another Bengali speaking State.

25. **Geeta Chattopadhyay** : (1941) Born in Kolkata. First book was published in 1973.

26. **Bhaskar Chakrabarty** : (1945) Born in Kolkata. First book published in 1971. Teacher by profession.

27. **Debarati Mitra** : (1946) Born in Kolkata. First book was published in 1971.

28. **Amitava Gupta** : (1947) Born in Kolkata. First book published in 1970. Written book on post modern poetry. Teacher English in a Kolkata college.

29. **Krishna Basu** : (1947) Born in Chandannagar, West Bengal. First book was published in 1976. A distinct woman voice in support of feminist writing. Teacher Bengali in a Kolkata college.

30. **Ranajit Das** : (1949) Born in Silchar, Assam, graduated from Guahati University. First book was published in 1977. Works with the State Government.

31. **Tushar Chaudhury** : (1949) Born in Kolkata. First book was published in 1976. Edited little magazine *Kabita Darpan*. Works with Central Government.

32. **Parthapratim Kanjilal** : (1949) Born in Kolkata. First book was published in 1970. Working with State Government.

33. **Shyamalkanti Das** : (1951) Born in Midnapur. First book was published in 1952. Edited atleast ten little magazines in various phases. Edited various poetry anthologies in Bengali. Edited a collection of essays on Satyajit Ray. Works as an associate editor of *Anandamela*, a fortnightly magazine for children.

34. **Joy Goswami** : (1954) Born in Ranaghat, a district town, now settled in Kolkata. First book was published in 1977. Received Akademi award for his poetry book *Paagli Tomar Sange* (With you, the unrestrained) in 2000. Visited Iowa

in 2001 in writers exchange programme. Also written novels. Works with *Desh*, a fortnightly Bengali literary magazine.

35. **Dhiman Chakrabarty** : (1954) Born in Kolkata. First book was published in 1989. Edited little magazine *Kabita Campus* and later *Aalap* both on poetry. Joint editor of Post modern Bengali poetry. Works with a nationalised Bank.

36. **Punnyasloke Dasgupta** : (1955) Born in North Bengal. His first book was published during late seventies. Runs his own business in Dhupguri.

37. **Mridul Dasgupta** : (1955) Born in West Bengal. First book published in 1980. Remained associated with various little magazine movements specially the anti-establishment movements. By profession a journalist with a Bengali daily news paper *Aajkal*.

38. **Subodh Sarkar** : (1957) First collection was published in 1980. Editor of the little magazine *Bhasanagar* which worked as a bridge between Bengali poetry and poetry of other languages in translation. Teaches English in a Kolkata college. Visited USA during early nineties to work with Allen Ginsberg and in Taiwan during 1995 to participate in Asian Poet, Conference.

39. **Sanjukta Bandopadhyay** : (1958) Born at Bally, Howrah District. First book was published in 1982. By profession a librarian in a school.

40. **Aneek Rudra** : (1959) Born in Bankura district of West Bengal. First book was published in 1986. Associated with and is in the editorial board of a number of little magazines. Doctorate in pharmaceutical sciences, a school teacher.

41. **Pinaki Thakur** : (1959) Born in Hooghly. First book published in 1994. Working with leading Bengali magazine *Desh*.

43. **Mallika Sengupta** : (1960) First book was published in 1983. A strong feminist voice, she visited Sweden and Australia as a part of Indian Writers' Delegation. Teaches sociology in a Kolkata college and associated with editing poetry in a Bengali fortnightly commercial magazine.

44. **Prabal Kumar Basu** : (1960) Born in Kolkata. First book published in 1983. Edited little magazines named *Alimpan, Satkarni* and acted as guest editor of various special numbers. A strong proponent of revival of verse drama and a pioneer of stage production of Bengali poetry. By profession an engineer working with a multinational company.

45. **Joydeb Basu** : (1962) Born in Kolkata. First book was published in 1989. He is an active member of the communist party and a lecturer in Bengali in a Kolkata college.

46. **Rahul Purakayastha** : (!963) Born in Kolkata. First book published in 1988. Media person by profession.

47. **Rupak Chakrabarty** : (1965) First book was published in 1999. Associated with a bimonthly Bengali magazine published from the United States.

48. **Chiranjib Basu** : (1968) Born in and represents the youngest generation of twentieth century poetry. First booklet was published in 1997. Edits a poetry magazine named *Kobikatha.* Associated with an Airlines company.

49. **Bibhas Roychaudhury** : **(1969)** Born in North 24 Parganas. First book was published in 1999.

50. **Mandakranta Sen** : (1972) First book was published in 1999. Apart from poetry also writes prose and has novels and verse drama to her credit. Edits little magazine *Brishtidin.*

50. **Mandakranta Sen** : (1972) First book was published in 1999. Apart from poetry also writes prose and has novels and verse drama to her credit. Edits little magazine *Brishtidin*.

THE ARTISTS

Somenath Hore. Born 1921 in Chittagong, now Bangladesh. Studied in Govt. College of Art and Craft, Kolkata, 1945-49. National awards: 1960, 1962, 1963. Gagan Aban Award, Visva Bharati 1985. Abanindra Puraskar by Govt. of West Bengal 1995. Former Principal, Kala Bhavana, Santiniketan.

K.G. Subramanyan. Born 1924 in Kerala. Studied at Kala Bhavana, Santiniketan. Scholar at Slade School of Art 1955-56. JDR Third Fund Fellowship to USA 1966-67. Gagan Aban Award, Visva Bharati. Professor Emeritus, Visva Bharati. Kalidas Samman.

Sanat Kar. Born 1936. Studied in Government College of Art and Craft 1950-55. Member, Society of Contemporary Artists, Kolkata. Exhibited in India and abroad. Former Principal, Kala Bhavana, Visva Bharati.

Ganesh Haloi. Born 1936, Jamalpur, Bengal. Studied in Government College of Art and Craft, Kolkata. Exhibited in India and abroad. Latham Foundation Award, USA. Shiromani Puraskar, Kolkata.

Ganesh Pyne. Born 1937, Kolkata. Studied in Government College of Art and Craft, Kolkata 1955-59. Exhibited all over India and abroad. Shiromani Puraskar, Kolkata 1997. Gagan Aban Award, Visva Bharati.

Jogen Chowdhury. Born 1939, Faridpur, Bengal. Studied in Government College of Art and Craft, Kolkata 1955-60. L' Ecole des Beaux Arts, Paris 1965-67. Award in Havanna Biennal. Shiromani Puraskar, Kolkata. Kalidas Samman. Former Principal, Kala Bhavana, Visva Bharati.

Tapas Konar. Born 1953. Studied in Indian College of Art, Kolkata 1975-80. Exhibitions in India and abroad including show in Esther Schoo's Gallery, Amsterdam.

Jaya Ganguly. Born 1958, Kolkata. Studied in Indian College of Art 1975-80. Birla Academy Award, Kolkata. Exhibited all over India and abroad, including Art of Bengal, CIMA and Esther Schoo's Gallery, Amsterdam.

GLOSSARY

Subhas Mukhopadhyay

Lakshmi — Hindu Goddess of wealth

Aladin — A character from the Arabian Nights story 'Aladin And The Magic Lamp' where Aladin has a lamp which can call down a genie who can work wonders for Aladin.

Rama And Lakshmana — The hero of the Hindu epic Ramayana and his younger brother.

Birendra Chattopadhyay

River Gangaur — Mythological sacred river

Behula — Mythological character in the popular ballads of Manasa, the snake Goddess, who kills her husband Lakhinder to force his father, Chand the merchant, to worship Manasa, a new entrant to the pantheon. Behula bears her husband's corpse to the gods in a long journey on a raft, and reclaims his life.

Arun Sarkar

Rakta Kingshuk — Crimson flowers of spring and summer

Nirendranath Chakrabarty

Dhoti — The traditional loin cloth worn by men in India.

Chowringhee — An affluent residential and commercial neighbourhood along the sprawling Maidan, Kolkata's largest patch of greenery, and heart of Kolkata's European district.

Manindra Gupta

Shomi tree	A tree of the acacia species, with a Mahabharata association, as the tree in which the Pandavas hid their weapons when they were driven to exile.
Narad	Mythological sage and also a messenger of the gods who was given to carrying tales and inciting and enjoying quarrels among gods.

Shankha Ghosh

Santhali	Of the Santhals, a tribe living in Midnapur, Birbhum and other districts of West Bengal

Shakti Chattopadhyay

Jarasandha	A Mahabharata character, born in two parts of two mothers, was joined togather by the ogress, Jara; hence named Jarasandha, i.e. joined by Jara.
Jara	Decrepitude, also name of the ogress in the Mahabharata.
Roro	River flowing by Chaibasa, Singhbhum District, Jharkhand.
Nimtala	One of the cremation grounds for the dead in Kolkata. Rabindranath Tagore was cremated here.

Sunil Gangopadhyay

Sealdah	Railway Station in central Kolkata which sheltered a horde of refugees after the partition of India.
Amlaki	Emblica, Emblic myrobalan
Darga -Satyapir	Tomb of the dervish Satya, the popular belief goes that a wish is fulfilled if something precious is offered to the sacred edifice.

Samarendra Sengupta

Manabendra Roy	M.N. Roy (1887-1954), Bengali member of the Communist International and associate and critic of Lenin; later founder and leader of the Radical Humanist movement in India.
Benoy	Benoy Mazumder, contemporary poet and cult figure.
Jibanananda	Jibanananda Das (1899-1954), eminent modern Bengali poet.
Metiabruz	A predominantly industrial west Calcutta locality inhabited by industrial and working class.
Kabita Sinha	Eminent Bengali poet and author (1931-1995)

Amitava Dasgupta

Sundari	A kind of timber tree that grows in the swamps of the Sunderbans
Garan	The mangrove or its timber
Bhakra Nangal	One of the major dams of India located at the Punjab.
Balaram	Elder brother to Lord Krishna
Gangotri	A holy place of the Hindus in the Garhwal hills. Flowing through this place the Ganges comes down to the plains.
Odissi	A classical dance form of Orissa
Santhali Madal	A percussion instrument of the Santhals
Bhangra	A popular Punjabi folk dance
Mudra	Any pose or gesture in classical Indian dance
Bharat Natyam	Popular classical dance form of South India

Mehfil	An informal gathering where classical songs and / or dances are performed for a select audience
Babri	Controversial mosque in Uttar Pradesh which is believed to have been built by Babar, the first Mughal emperor of India. This mosque was demolished in 1992 by a section of people who believe that there is a Hindu temple underneath.
Sarpunthi	Type of small fish which when cooked is a delicacy for the Bengalis.

Utpal Kumar Basu

Suren Banerjee Road	Major road in central Kolkata named after Surendranath Banerjea who led the protests against the proposed partition of Bengal in the early twentieth century.
Dubulia	A health resort in Bihar.
Rashid Ali day	A day of political demonstrations, violent protest and police reprisal in Kolkata, demanding the release of Capt. Rashid Ali of the Indian National Army.

Pranabendu Dasgupta

Jatin Bagchi	Bengali poet (1878-1948)

Tarapada Ray

Sundarban	Dense forest in West Bengal, famous for Royal Bengal tigers
Gir forest	Forest in Gujrat known for its lion population.

Shaktipada Brahmachari

Chaitra	One of the summer months of the Bengali calendar
Acharya	Guru or preceptor of a particular discipline.

Vijaya Mukhopadhyay

Lanka	Sri Lanka
Sita	Wife of Lord Rama in the epic Ramayana
Ayodhya	Capital of Rama's empire
Pushpak	Flying chariot, believed to be the carrier of Indra, the king of gods in Hindu mythology
Raghupati	Another name of Rama
Raghubhamsha	Long poem by Kalidasa (between 300 – 500 A.D.), giving a chronological account of the dynasty of Raghu.

Monibhushan Bhattacharya

Amritabazar	Once popular Bengali daily newspaper
Anandabazar	Popular Bengali daily newspaper
Lalgola passenger	Slow train whose destination is Lalgola, a remote place in Murshidabad near the border of Bangladesh
Ghoogni	Delicious snack made from whole gram
Farakka	Dam on river Ganges, supplies water to both Bangladesh and West Bengal
Punjabi	Loose upper garment worn by both men and women
Statesman	Popular English daily newspaper
Kurukshetra	Famous battlefield in the epic Mahabharata where the two adversaries Pandavas and Kauravas fought for the throne of Hastinapur
Babus	The elite middle class Bengali
Subhadra	Sister of Balaram and Lord Krishna
D.I.B	District Investigation Branch

Geeta Chattopadhyay

Aalta	A red watery substance to outline the feet used as a part of bridal make-up by Bengali women. The classical idea of beauty holds this as symbolising blushing feet.
Ghat	The steps leading to any water body, pond, river.
Dog	Accompanied Yudhistir on his journey to Heaven
Yudhistir	Eldest of the Pandavas in the Mahabharata, who is believed to have ascended to Heaven.
Baitarini	A river which is believed to be the border between earth and heaven in Hindu mythology.

Bhaskar Chakrabarty

Noolia	Natives who help the uninitiated to take a bath in the sea, particularly along the eastern coast of India.

Debarati Mitra

Keya	A monsoon flower
Sraban	One of the two rainy months in the Bengali calendear

Amitava Gupta

Arjun	The third brother of the Pandavas and also the Champion warrier in the epic Mahabharata
Kunti	Mother of the Pandavas
Karna	The illegitimate son of Kunti fathered by the Sun God
Krishna	Hindu God who in the Mahabharata was Arjun's charioteer in the Kurukshetra war.

Krishna Basu

Sindoor	Vermilion powder applied on hair parting by married Hindu women.
Sankha	Bangles made of conch shell customarily worn by married Hindu women.
Asur	Mythic antagonist of the Hindu gods.
Khoai	Raft terrain around Santiniketan
Benarasi	Type of gorgeous long piece of silk usually worn by Bengali women as a wedding dress.

Tushar Chaudhury

Atar	Indian perfume generated from the state Uttarpradesh.
Hari	Another name for lord Krishna.
Sonkha and Chakra	Conch-shell and discus adorning two hands of Lord Narayana, a Hindu God
Monu	According to myth one of the fourteen sons of Brahma (the absolute being). Regarded as the father and first law giver of mankind.

Shyamalkanti Das

Bankura	A district town of West Bengal.
Jessore, Khulna and Haridaspur.	Once important towns in the undivided Bengal, now part of Bangladesh.

Joy Goswami

Tamal	A big tree of the Palm variety, under which Lord Krishna used to meet his beloved Radha. Hence a symbol of love.

Subodh Sarkar

Gandhi	M.K. Gandhi (1869 - 1948) recognised as the Father of the Nation, who led India during the freedom movement following non-violence principles and was assassinated soon after Independence.
Pupul Jayakar	Close associate of Gandhi, and later popularizer of handicrafts.
Rajghat	Place in Delhi where Gandhi was cremated and subsequently a monument was built
Yamuna	River of North India flowing through Delhi
Teenmurti	First official residence of the Prime Minister of India
Astamangala	The Bengali custom of the return of the bride and the groom to the bride's home after eight days of marriage.
Sari	Five and half meter long piece of cloth usually worn by Indian women.

Sanjukta Bandyopadhyay

Maidan	A long stretch of greenery at the heart of Kolkata

Aneek Rudra

Rajma	Type of lentil
Espahan Bukhara	Two pre-historic places in Iran, which became the cultural centre in those days.
Gandhara Art	The art of north–western India, marked by a strong Greek influence, particularly in its sculpture.
Vishnu	Hindu God

Pinaki Thakur

Probashi	People domiciled outside their native place
Tabla	Percussion Instrument
Esraj	String Instrument
Palash	Crimson flowers of spring and summer

Mallika Sengupta

Chitrangada	Princess of Manipur, consort of Arjuna in the epic Mahabharata; the leading character of a long verse drama, Chitrangada by Rabindranath Tagore.
Draupadai	The name of the heroine of Mahabharata as she was the daughter of the king Drupada.
Shivalinga	A phallic symbol of Shiva, one of the three principal Hindu Gods.

Prabal Kumar Basu

Korma	Delicious Bengali non-vegetarian dish

Joydev Basu

Mandar	Heavenly tree
Roja	Holy fastings of the Muslims from sunrise to sundown during the month of Ramadan
Amrit	Nectar, a mythological elixir fabled to make man immortal.
Praharas	Hours of the day by ancient computation

Namaz	Daily prayer of the Muslims
Arwal	A particularly backward part of Bihar, scene of caste battles
Brahmarshi	A Brahman sage

Rahul Purakayastha

Maya	Illusion, a reference to mayavad which maintains that the whole created world is an illusion.
Chou	Folk dance form of rural Bengal, Bihar and Orissa

Rupak Chakrabarty

Gitabitan	The collection of songs of Tagore.

Bibhas Roychaudhury

Padma	Major river of Bangladesh
Kalmi	Type of edible aquatic plant
Baul	One of a class of Hindu stoical devotees singing songs in a special mode illustrating their doctrine.
Bidi	A local cigarette

Mandakranta Sen

Shahid Minar	Monuments of Martyrs in Kolkata, scene of all social and political rallies